FOREVER YOURS

FOREVER YOURS!

THE UNPUBLISHED WORKS

LYRICS AND POEMS

OF

TONY ROSE

1966 - 2016

FOREVER YOURS!

THE UNPUBLISHED WORKS

LYRICS AND POEMS

OF

TONY ROSE

1966 - 2016

AMBER BOOKS

PHOENIX/LOS ANGELES/NEW YORK CITY

FOREVER YOURS
Published by:
Amber Books
An Imprint of Amber Communications Group, Inc.
1334 East Chandler Boulevard, Suite 5-D67
Phoenix, Arizona 85048
amberbk@aol.com
www.amberbooks.com

Tony Rose / Publisher, Editor and Editorial Director
Yvonne Rose, Associate Publisher / Senior Editor
Quality Press, Production Coordinator/Book Packager
www.qualitypress.info

ALL RIGHTS RESERVED

No parts of this book may be reproduced or transmitted in any form or by any means electronic or mechanical, including photocopying, recording or any information storage and retrieved system without the written permission from the authors, except for the inclusion of brief quotations in a review.

This is a work of fiction. Names, characters, businesses, places, events, locales, and incidents are either the products of the author's imagination or used in a fictitious manner. Any resemblance to actual persons, living or dead, or actual events is purely coincidental.

Copyright © by Conant B. Rose
Paperback ISBN #: 978-1-937269-88-3
Library of Congress Control Number: 2018947964

DEDICATION

Forever Yours, a book of unpublished works, words, poems and lyrics, is dedicated to *Yvonne Rose* for her Inspiration, friendship, love, and dedicated service, as my muse, best friend, wife, and lover, for almost forty years.

TABLE OF CONTENTS

DEDICATION i

TABLE OF CONTENTS iii

PREFACE v

THE 1960's 1

THE 1970's 19

The 1980's 89

The 1990's 149

THE 2000's 179

THE 2010's 191

THE JOURNEY OF LIFE IS EVERYTHING 195

TONY ROSE BOOK CATALOG AND MUSIC DISCOGRAPHY 203

TONY ROSE BOOKS AND MUSIC 204

PREFACE

When I was thirteen I saw the Beatles on the Ed Sullivan show and I immediately picked up a broom and imitated them playing something that was in their hands. Some-time later, I learned that what they had in their hands was called a guitar.

Once I learned what it was and what it was called and that you could buy one, I looked in the Sears and Roebuck catalog, and saw a picture of what a guitar looked like. It looked exactly like what the Beatles had in their hands when I saw them on the Ed Sullivan Show.

The catalog said it cost $39.99, so I immediately started saving for it. I was working at the Christian Scientist Monitor Newspaper in the afternoons after school, and selling the Record American Newspaper at night, and the Bay State Banner on the weekends. I was a professional Newspaper boy and had been one since I was six years old.

Within two months I was standing at the loading dock of the Sears and Roebuck store, across from a park called The Fenway, and about one mile from the Whittier Street Housing Projects where I lived, with my arms outstretched, reaching up, while the warehouse guy lowered down my box with my bright red, shiny, new guitar in it.

The world shifted for me at that moment because I knew just what I wanted to do. I took that guitar home and right away I started plucking the strings, singing to it, making up words, my hand doing what the Beatles had done.

The guitar didn't sound like the Beatles did, but I had fun making up words and strumming my guitar. I did that for a couple of years and by the time I was fifteen I was rhyming and making up words to the songs I was listening to on my little am/fm radio, by James Brown, Major Lance, The Moments, The Delphonics, Marvin Gaye, The Four Tops, The Supremes, The Marvelettes, Mary Wells and all the English groups I was listening to like, The Beatles, The Rolling Stones, The Kinks, the Zombies, The Animals, Gerry and the Pacemakers, all the hits and hit-makers from the early sixties.

By the time I was sixteen I was given a book by some people in a school for truants, dropouts and at risk kids that I was going to at the time.

The book was called 'Black Voices'. It was an anthology of poems and short stories by black poets and writers, like, Sterling A. Brown, Charles W. Chesnutt, John Henrik Clarke, Countee Cullen, Frederick Douglass, Paul Laurence Dunbar, James Weldon Johnson, Naomi Long Madgett, Paule Marshall, Clarence Major, Claude McKay, Ann Petry, Dudley Randall, J. Saunders Redding, Jean Toomer, Darwin T.Turner, James Baldwin, Richard Wright, Langston Hughes, Ralph Ellison, Leroy Jones, W.E.B. Dubois, Gwendolyn Brooks, and Malcolm X.

It was the first time I had seen or read a book like this with all African American writers and poets and it literally changed my entire life. I, by this time, had read thousands of books from the bookmobile that used to come around the projects every week, and the libraries that I had taken a liking to for the books and as a place of refuge, whenever I needed a break from my mother and the ghetto.

I would go to the Roxbury Boys Club Library on Dudley Street, to the YMCA Book Library on Huntington Avenue, I read books everywhere in school and out of school, but never had I read stories and poems like these. I had a small bookcase, in my bedroom filled with books like: Robin Hood, the biography of John J. Audubon, King Arthur and the Round Table, Peter Pan,

Treasure Island, and the biography of Robert Louis Stevenson, but the stories and poems in 'Black Voices' were about me, and I was never the same again.

I began to see the world and approach the world differently, it was as if I had been awakened and was now aware of who I was and who we, as black people, are. I was now ready to begin my journey and knew that I wanted to be a writer or a journalist and that my guitar was a part of that. By the time I was seventeen I realized that I didn't know a damn thing about music.

But, I did know how to play what I heard and thought, and I could make up words that sounded like the guitar. I had never had a music lesson and I finally had realized, (some kid had told me), that the reason why my guitar didn't sound like the Beatles was because I needed an amplifier, but nobody in my family had known enough to tell me that and I didn't know.

But I soldiered on and began saying things to my guitar that I knew about, drinking, drugs and girls, making up stories and poetry about life in the ghetto. Just like my 'Black Voices' book, except with music and words that I made up.

By the time I was eighteen years old I had left the projects for Lackland Air Force Base and Shephards Air Force Base in Texas, Misawa Air Force Base in Japan, Puson Air Force Base in South Korea, Tegu Air Force Base in South Korea and DaNang Air Force base in South Vietnam. I wrote no poems or words when I was there, I was too busy being a warrior for good ole Lyndon Baines Johnson and then Richard Milhouse Nixon.

When I came home I got married; but I had no poems, no words for that marriage, until much later, when it was all over. But I did take creative writing classes, as an English Literature Major, and I did win short story writing awards, for two stories I wrote, *"And I will take the Clouds Clean out of The Sky and Give Them to You with Love"* and a story about my father, six dead people, and a place called N.E.G.R.O., called *"The Life",* while attending the University of Massachusetts (Boston). They were major accomplishments for me, at the time.

I then went to Los Angeles, where I found a guitar in Mexico and the words found me again. I met a woman who after she heard me say the words, on a guitar, put me in show business.

I found a friend in the mail room at Warner Brothers and Columbia pictures called The Burbank Studios, and we would sneak inside one of the screening rooms during lunchtime and I would write lyrics while he would play piano, giving notes to the chords that I would play on the piano for him.

It would be the first time I would write music and lyrics with somebody. Somehow that led to my being hired at Warner/Electra/Atlantic Records, (WEA) where someone thought I would do well to learn record distribution, marketing, accounting and sales.

Then RCA Records hired me and I was trained in studio record production, music business, marketing, promotion, distribution, and A&R work for the company.

I kept writing lyrics and music while I worked with Cuba Gooding, Sr. and Luther Simmons, members of RCA's biggest R&B group, The Main Ingredient, while managing, producing and writing for acts I signed to the RCA Records and the Main Ingredient's production company, Super Group Productions.

I went to work at night on Sunset Blvd. for a public relations firm owned by an African American man named Warren Lanier who showed me how to understand what public relations meant, and how to write press releases, and editorial copy for newspapers and magazines.

I booked and managed other acts like Shirley Hemphill at the Comedy Store and bands at other Hollywood and Beverly Hills nightclubs, from my Nova production offices on Hollywood Blvd. in Los Angeles, while taking acting lessons, music composition and creative writing courses at Los Angeles City College and attending the University of California at Los Angeles, eventually getting a B.A. in English Literature.

A few years later I returned to Boston and met a Boston Conservatory of Music graduate. We would take some courses at the New England Conservatory of Music together, and I would have a lot of music and words for her, mostly about space, galaxies, and universes.

A year or so later I would meet Maurice Starr, and get him a record deal with RCA Records, for a song he had out called *'Bout Time I Funk You Girl'*, and he would introduce me to a young musician named Charles Alexander. We would call ourselves Prince Charles and the City Beat Band; and Maurice, his brother Michael Johnzon, Prince Charles and I would make some words and music and I would have my first hit record, *"In the Streets"*, and go on to manage and produce, Prince Charles Alexander for the next ten years,

I would begin a record company called, Solid Platinum Records and Productions. We were very successful having production deals on Virgin Records, Atlantic Records and Pavilion - CBS/Sony Records, with licensing and co-publishing deals with many music companies in Europe, Canada, and the United States, sold some millions of records around the world, receiving two gold albums.

We wrote and published, words and music, like, Stone Cold Killers, Combat Zone, More Money, City Life, Cash Money, Big Chested Girls, Fistful of Dollars, Bush Beat, Rise, You Are My Love, Video Freak, Don't Fake the Funk, Tight Jeans and Skintight

Tina, from the albums "Gangwar", "Stone Killers" and "Combat Zone", songs about the ghetto, politics, money, sex and drugs, things we grew up with, loved, and knew very well

Some years later, I worked with Maurice Starr on a New Kids on the Block album and received two more gold and platinum albums and two ampex golden reel awards.

My words and music with Prince Charles and the City Beat Band and the other groups I wrote for, are still played, bought, sold and listened to on YouTube.com, Amazon.com, iTunes.com, Google.com, Unidisc.com, Cdbaby.com, and every music source throughout the world, to this very day, this very second.

That same year of, 1979, shortly after I had met Prince Charles Alexander and Maurice Starr, I met a muse named Yvonne, who attached herself to me, and became my inspiration.

Forever Yours, a book of unpublished works, words, poems and lyrics, is dedicated to Yvonne Rose for her friendship, love, and dedicated service, as my muse, wife, best friend and lover, for thirty-seven years.

I had enjoyed writing words, poems and lyrics since I was a young teenager. One day, once upon a time in a magical place, I married my muse, and during my early life, downtime from Prince Charles and the City Beat Band and upcoming life, I wrote, over the years, hundreds of these unpublished words, lyrics, and poems about 'love, life, and living', a lot of them about her, even before I had met her, and long after.

After the music writing and lyric years, I became a book publisher and author, with the number one African American book publishing company in the world, writing six international-critically acclaimed-best-selling books: *Is Modeling for You? The Handbook and Guide for the Aspiring Black Model; African*

American History in the United States of America; Before the Legend: The Rise of New Kids on the Block and a Guy Named Maurice Starr; How to be In the Entertainment Business and Become a Record Producer, Record Company, Personal Manager, Film Producer, and Book Publisher, A Beginners Guide to Success in the Music, Film, Television and Book Publishing Industries; The Autobiography of an American Ghetto Boy; America the Black Point of View; The Investigation of the White People of America and Western Europe and the Autobiography of an American Ghetto Boy; and *The Investigation of the White People of America and Western Europe,* bought, sold and read all over the world on YouTube.com, Amazon.com, Barnes and noble.com, iTunes.com, Google.com, and Amberbookspublishing.com.

I would publish over two hundred book titles, receiving among other accolades, many *Book Publisher of the Year Awards* and winning an *NAACP Image Award for Outstanding Literature*, and setting up a company, Quality Press in 2001, that to date has made authors and publishers of many thousands of African American writers.

I would complete, during my lifetime, a 380 degree turn around from the music world back to the world of books and writing books, a promise that I had made to myself decades ago, when I had to make a conscientious decision to change from the writing and journalism world to the music world.

Thank you for reading volume one of my unpublished works, words, lyrics, and poems. I hope that you enjoy them.

Forever Yours!

Tony Rose
April 6, 2018

THE 1960'S

FIFTEEN YEARS OLD

"If you don't know what I mean, then you can't have a meaning for what you don't know, understand."

- Fredro

FADE OUT IN A DREAM

I woke up to standing room only, after I had been washed ashore by them waves, but it was a little too late to go into that song and dance routine, after all, everybody and nobody had seen that.

So I proceeded to stand there and glare, I might have exposed myself, if I hadn't decided that I might repulse them as they repulsed me and thus lose my identity of being the only one to feel this sense of nausea, which is actually very pleasing to those of us who must face this sort of thing all the time.

It does get kind of depreciating to have to be bombarded with all this and more; still though, I seem to feel that my relationship with the throngs might somehow be of some good.

You know I was just thinking the other day, how good it was to have attained this high position in life.

After I thought it I had to burst out laughing from the sheer actuality of having thought that.

I could have gone into shock, might have too, but then that knock came on the door, and I was pulled under by Channel #5, Jean Nate bath oil and Norform Douche Tablets.

After all of that I decided to skip the day and retain my sense of depression by just farting through it.

Which is something I seem to do very well, you know I farted through one day a total of 293 times, I might have a world's record or something, I don't know. You know all this black awareness is getting to me, all the time having to be aware.

And talk about everyday nothings! Unconsciously I awoke to a screaming thought that maybe it was I who had dreamt this nothing of life, but so would others, I'm not alone here!

There are millions who dream, nothing happens, but still life goes on.

It's made to happen that way. I know it doesn't seem as though all this could possibly be happening, I hope not because if all this tranquility is real, then what are we being so desperate about?

I know, it must be the scene we're in today, act 1, act 2, act 3, etc., and all that, yet we try to play it through, because it's fun having to live.

And you know that to be true! It really is, if it wasn't you would be dead and not really existing in your mind and ways.

No! It's not so, not if you want to believe you're really dead, extremes and all them hardship cases of pure soul.

Ha, it's hell now? Wait until you can count the screaming few, who'll really be existing for a cause, if there are any left to speak of.

And while you're waiting for whatever it is you're waiting for, try not to think how long you've been waiting for it.

You might actually die before it comes, but, there must be lots of things to do in this mind of ours, that's what it is you know.

Yeah, it's just a mind and you're trapped right in yourself, engraved forever with you, ha, ha, poor soul, that's too bad. But, I've got mine too, forever! Rewards sometimes come too late!

You know! It must have surprised a lot of people when you started with them long steeples.

And how did you feel when they weren't surprised anymore 'cause, you were strung out and dead.

And whatever for and what for, did we do that for, I mean, it wasn't even cool, not really, but!

But, you know all those un-together times, doing it, doing you, to me and dyyyyyyyyying to boot and then not wanting to return, to an unrealistic realism.

And you thought that you had won, and you wasn't even yourself, because you wasn't cool, at the time.

Fredro
Conant B. Rose © 1966

PRELUDE TO CONVERSATIONS

Not too loud, brothers and sisters, least, the man hear you, (like he usually does)

You're bad, keep cool, don't be no fool, just because you didn't go to school

I mean, like, you have to have, some intelligence (to drop out)

Wow, you're a real super cool, your sister pimps your mother

And you tried your dog, girls, in parks, elevators, alleys, hallways,

And in my bathtub.

Issac's a cool alcoholic, found dead with a transistor radio around his neck

And a bottle of T Bird wine in his left back pocket

Wow, like a good fuck, is to lay and lay and lay it on her

Wow, great, but can you do it to her real good?

Thighs, mound, legs, breast, hair, face,

Her body actions and make-believe love, with sweat, sweating.

Wow! Over, you want to sleep, she wants to talk about her mother

Filled her body with mines and now she wants to talk about her mother

Fredro
Conant B. Rose © 1967

CONVERSATIONS

Tired heart, tired people, tired longings, with overdue payments, on living expenses.

On someone else's time.

Gregory

Jackson

Ty

Gerald

Amil

Deggie

Issac

Shelia

And many, many others, have all died in 1967. This is one night out of their lives, they, could not survive.

Setting - any steps, everyone is high or trying to get high. It is about 10:30pm and it is a summer night. They will have between them .39 cents, it is all about nothing and tonight they will realize that.

Scene – Steps in Grove Hall - 10:30pm

Jackson - *Jesus is coming. He's going to...*

Gerald - You ain't nothing Ty, you ain't no good, you ain't even going to do what you said, you ain't shit Ty.

Ty - (Laughing) Are you taking my name in vain. Ty Yi, Ty Yi.

Jackson - I do believe that he's the one, my man! You know I used to....

Fredro

Conant B. Rose © 1967

MORE CONVERSATIONS

Amel - (He has on a long flowing multi-colored dashiki, with pink silk underwear on underneath, while sipping wine) - *This wine tastes bad, you know they even selling bad wine to us. Black people ought to.........*

Gerald - (High Already) - *Kill them motherfuckers.* (nods again)

Ty - (Singing to himself and humming and looking around, looks at Deggie, who's talking with Issac.)

Deggie - *Ha, ha, you was cool, when you wasn't high, ha, ha, look at you now, you look out there.*

Issac - (Scratching his thigh, eyes rolling down) - *Your mother was out there to last night, she was highhhhhh.*

Ty - *Ty Yi* (still looking at Deggie) - *Hey piss, pass me some wine!*

Deggie - (Taking another sip of wine, some of it dribbles down his chin) - *Fuck you!*

Shelia - (While scratching her stomach) - *You must have forgot why I was here.*

Gerald - *You want some dizope man? or is you high already on Jesus.*

Amel - *That white Jesus.*

Deggie - *In drag. Ha.*

Jackson - (Slowly smiling and looking exalted) *Bump you, you clowns, that's why all of you are nothing, nothing!*

Because you can't be something and always be thinking of nothing, there must be something you think about
You! You, Ty, what do you think about.

Ty - Another note (What he thought about all the time, is of course as American as apple pie, but due to environmental control, we choose to censure it).

(All in Chorus)

Amel - *Shut up!* (Violent all of a sudden, he doesn't even realize why) - *Shut up, you stupid motherfuckers. Jackson's right, what do we think about! Dope! How high we can get?* (tone rising) - *Yeah, that's all, this is it, all of it. We're nothing but shadowless prints, implanted and embedded right here on these steps, we've always been here and we'll always be here, until someone guesses how really useless we are and removes us.*

Gregory - *And how high are you, brother.* (Gregory had been sitting, just sitting, not moving or speaking, Gregory has been thinking thoughts into this conversation, for he knows its talkers are as useless to themselves, as society is useless to them).

Amel - (Amel turns and looks upward towards the back and top of the steps where Gregory's voice came from. As he turns, he's puzzled by the seemingly unemotional, but angry sound in Gregory's voice and wonders what prompted him to speak as such)

Shelia - (Throughout this short and endless nothing, Shelia has become sick. Nobody pays attention to her as she throws up over the side of the steps)

Issac - *You alright, Shelia* (Issac out of his nod, notices Shelia's plight, and realizes he might cop some.)

Shelia - *Yeah, help me to the back Issac.*

Issac - *Sure baby* (Shelia and Issac move to the back to shoot up. Junkies make love to dope, not each other.)

Gregory - *Everybody here is going nowhere, why don't we just kill each other, it's quicker than just sinking away.*

Ty - *We are killing each other, but you first.*

Hunter - *Let's go in the back and get Shelia, I saw her go in the back with Issac.* (Ty, Petey, Hunter and Deggie go towards the shadows.)

Amel - *Ain't you going back there too Greg?*

Gregory - *Naw, I spent two months going back and forth to the clinic because of her.*

Amel - *Ha, ha, and they all gone back there, to her.* (Amel and Gregory laugh together)

Act 2

(There isn't nothing in existence)

We're a joke, a great big complex joke, not allowed to laugh.

We can't be real, not now, not again, not here.

We should have been extinct decades ago, yet we still flourish, we're still abundant, still producing. Still wanting. Still hoping.

Still hoping to get some when there is nothing for us to get, it's already been used, it's came and begot.

There ain't nothing left for us. Why haven't we realized it yet? Because we don't want to, we have nowhere else to go, so we've decided to die here, without a struggle. We've also decided to help society along, if we have to die, and we must, we've decided to die cool and high.

Society labored us, so we allow you to wallow in us. You won't crumble, you're too strong, but you'll remember us with your decadence.

Society adapt yourself to us, not we to you, it's too late. We know there is nowhere for us to go, and I guess the majority of us have resigned ourselves to a slow nothing in death or a quick recovery in surviving.

It really all depends on how many of us are still strong enough to withstand all the drawbacks.

Act 3

Jackson - (looking at Greg and Amel, watching them laugh. Thinking of why they were still here and what drew him back each night, why was it he was laughed at all the time and looked down upon, just for his belief in something? Was it because they were scared to believe in anything else, as their earlier beliefs had gone into nothing.

Nobody had anything to contribute.

To have any hope or belief in their eyes meant leaving them behind, thus you have to be hated and scorned.

No, he thought, they already consider themselves dead. Maybe they are right. Maybe we as a people are dead.

All in Chorus.

Hold up the tradition, onward with action, before it's too late and we haven't lived a day.

(November 27, 1967, 104 murders in Black Boston, I knew some.)
Peace and love.
Fredro
Conant B. Rose – © 1967

THE WHITTIER STREET HOUSING PROJECTS IN ROXBURY (BOSTON), MA, WHERE I LIVED, GREW UP, AND BEGAN WRITING. WE LIVED ON THE FIFTH FLOOR STRAIGHT AHEAD.

THE PROJECTS AND JAIL

Red walled and useless to the eye and all that musky smell tearing and touching all through your imprisoned glob of flesh.

Standing up only, room only signs, and you, for the first time in what you know won't be the last time, make believe that you're not where you are;

Singing birds, green grass, lakes and girls and girls, and more shit than clouds can cover, forgetting you, and staring up and forgetting what you remembered;

Remembering where you are, clang, clang, doors clang tightly shut against you, protecting you from whatever they are protected from, and it smells so bad in here, and it's cold and dark.

And it's un-touching your touched eyes, from this perverted and distorted magnet that clings to your very body.

Fungus from the countless hollers and screams that have come in this very place where you now lay.

The walls close and so do your lids.

Wail sirens wail and bells ring and boots stomp and women and men scratch, moans are heard, toilets flush and doors clang.

Castle keepers are heard to shout, walls are creaking, orders are passed, men move about, you're watched by all that moves and what doesn't watches you, too.

You crunch and munch your scenery and you fill your glass of air, as you look up the ceiling reaches you, in one fast blinding motion, you remember, colors and shapes and sizes and smells and, and, you remember it all.

This place has no time and existence only has a color scheme; it's hell to pay for existing, the walls might gather your screams, and passing time is an endless adventure of endless corridors and thoughts which are recorded in a moment of time, by these very walls which record all that you look.

It measures your face and scans your movements and remembers your thoughts and laughs at your array of distortions; the floor falls back from you and you wait for whatever it is you're waiting for; you hear laughter and you feel as helpless as when you squat.

Forgiven already is tomorrow, for sure, you can't hate if there is nothing there to hate.

Stomp, boots stomp and you wonder if that was you or your echo.

Clang, doors clang shut, you lay and all the torments are piled on you.

The walls laugh as they reach inward and pull out the gray depressors, ah, how large they look, how somber they are, as they look at you, look at them, waiting for you.

Scurry, rats scurry, all over, and you wage a fierce good battle for your very existence in sanity; you dare not get up for fear of having company when you return.

The sun shines bright on my home and illuminates my cage.

I'm you, I am you, I say to the walls. I have known you and you have covered me and your stink in my breath, I am cold and no amount of hell can warm me. It is gray and images are less than shadows.

Turmoil and utter confusion reign behind those walls, hate is king, and lust is queen.

Suspicion is essential behind those walls, inside it is dark, it is a wasteful bondage to those who inhale it, unreality has no real greatness for the women and men and their prison.

If you listen hard enough with your eyes, you can see that the wall really does talk, sometimes you add in another voice that's in-sizzored in your brain for life.

Bree, whistles bree, lights glare all over the walls, blinding you, back and forth, covering all, missing no spot.

The walls whisper, whisper, whisper, doors will shut, men will riot;

The walls are alive now; it as not some electric source that aroused this condemned fortress;

The walls echo with shouts, from deep down they are coming, from deep down they start, until the roar crashes against the walls, until the noise is so deafening, as to make you realize the horror you are living.

And you lie, and you weep, and you remember; pretty, soft, music, slowly dancing, whispering creeping lakes, tranquility; and you hear shouts, walls, ceilings, bars, doors clang, and you scream and you hide behind the noise, and you rush, rush on.

Head, noise, walls, and you; masses, arms firing, and you scream, blood, red walled and useless to the eye and all that musky smell tearing, touching, all through your imprisoned glob of flesh, standing up only signs, and you for the last time make believe you're not where you are, and you then remember, you are who you are and remember.

Fredro

Conant B. Rose © 1968

HOME FOR CHRISTMAS LEAVE. LEAVING FOR JAPAN, SOUTH KOREA, VIETNAM, THE SAME DAY THIS PHOTO WAS TAKEN.

HEY BLACK PEOPLE

Hey! Black people, what you do in your own race in for

I mean we love life too, O, you talk of love and love one another

Unity in one cause for Hicks, man you dead, dead, dead

Rose love yourself, don't die. Can't die. Can't live either

In this world, kill him, before he kills you, Run cowards of night, curse your deeds

You motherfuckers of hells hopelessness, all cursed by your mother's deeds of shame

Live on, live on Rose, Give him your name, Rose

He loves to live, to give

Save us O race, save us O race, save us O race

A man died last night, why

Tears don't be shed for naught, and shame

Be torn, least you cry a bitch before you die and shit

Man who wants to live a life of shit and

Ahhhhhhhhhhhhhhhhhhhhhhhhhhhhhhh

God save the dope!

Fredro
Conant B. Rose © 1968

MY FIRST WIFE, BETTY JAYNE AND SON, CONANT, ROXBURY (BOSTON) MA, 1971

THE 1970'S

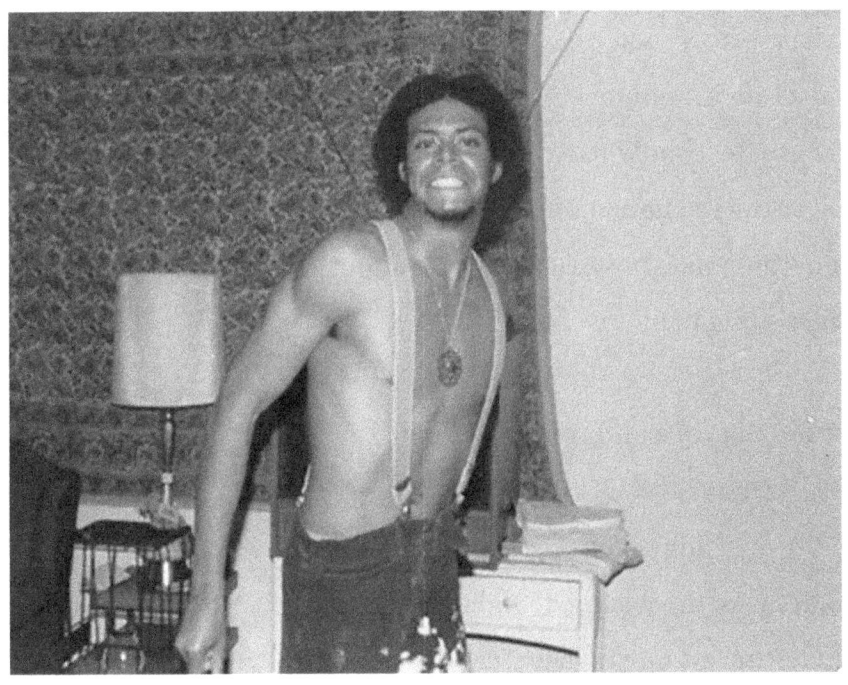

*TONY ROSE, 1245 VINE STREET,
HOLLYWOOD, CA, 1973*

HOLLYWOOD AND VINE

Hollywood and vine.
Make up your mind.
Going to the city, yeah.
And drink some wine.

Make me a winner, oh.
You know it's gonna be.
The greatest show in this city.
You know I'm gonna find me
Something nice now, OOOO, there's one in every crowd.
There's one in every crowd

I really dig rock and roll
I dig Barry White
I'll do anything to survive
Don't make me wrong or right
Cause, there's one in every crowd
There's one in every crowd.

Hollywood and Vine
Make up your mind.
Going to the city, yeah,
And drink some wine.

Make me a winner, oh.

You know It's gonna be.

The greatest show in this city.

You know I'm gonna find me,

Something nice, 000O,

There's one in every crowd

There's one in every crowd.

I really dig rock and roll

I love David Bowie

I'll do anything to get in.

Don't make me wrong or right

Cause, there's one in every crowd

There's one in every crowd

There's one in every crowd

Conant B. Rose © 1973

IT'S A WAY

Sometimes we're born to die, yeah
And sometimes we're born to survive
And sometimes we're born to live another day
But all of us know it's not right
Not right, not right, not right, at all
It's just a way

Sometimes we're here to be
And sometimes we're here to know
And sometimes we're just a little bit to late
But we all know it's not right no, no,
It's not right it's not right
It's just a way

Sometimes we become fanatics
Sometimes we don't even do that
And sometimes we wish we never knew
But it's still not right
Not right, not right, not right, at all
It's just a way

Yeah and some of us are desperate people
And some of us are made to order
And some of us realize the facts

But it's still not right, not right, no way

It's not right at all

It's just a way

Some of us graciously die

And still a few of us survive

But if we love

And I'm sure we'll love

And if we give

And I'm sure we'll give

And if we live, to give

Our love, one love

To all of us

Then I'm sure

That more than a few will know peace

And I'm sure that more than a few will not cease

Because the way it is,

It's just not right

Not right, not right, at all

It's just a way

Conant B. Rose © 1973

BEAUTY

Beauty, Oh beauty, have you seen the moon glow
Beauty, Oh beauty, have you seen the flowers grow
I didn't know oh beauty
Beauty, I didn't know you would go

Where are you now
What have you been doing
Who is your love this morning

Beauty, oh beauty how is it with you
Beauty, oh beauty i still love you so
Oh beauty I want to go away too
I didn't know Oh beauty, I didn't know you would go

Oh beauty it must have been love
Oh beauty I dream of heaven above
Oh beauty was it love

I just want to know what it is beauty
I just want to know why I cry
Why do my eyes search the sky
I remember all those nights we loved
I'd touch your face and kiss your mouth
Oh, what is left, Oh what is mine

Oh beauty I'll see you again in time

Oh beauty it must have been love

Oh beauty I dream of heaven above

Oh beauty was it love

I sit and watch the birds fly

I sometimes laugh I often cry

Oh beauty have you seen the flowers grow

Conant B. Rose © 1973

RUNNIN DOG BLUES

Look at me runnin to you, yeah
What can I do
I'm a fool dreaming of you
Oh, lord
I got the runnin dog blues

I got troubles, too alone in time
Got no time to be runnin you down
I got a feeling in my dealings
Down in my firebox
Just to be there looking at you
What can I do
I got the runnin dog blues

Why baby, I tired of being alone
I tired of making love to everyone but you
Come to me babe, and let my heart go crazy
I want to burn in big ways for you

Oh, baby, can't you see me now
Oh, baby, can't you look at me now
Oh, baby, don't you know

Oh

I got the runnin dog blues

Oh, yeah Oh, yeah

I got the runnin dog blues

Conant B. Rose © 1973

TONY ROSE, 1245 VINE STREET, HOLLYWOOD, CA 1973

LADY

Lady so fair, lady so blue
Wish I was there loving you

Lady so fair, lady so new
Are you the same or are you two
Wish I knew

Dream a little, dream a little, of me at night
Think of me always, I'll be alright

Lady so fair, lady so blue
Wish I was there loving you
Wish I was there dreaming with you
Wish I was there loving with you
Loving with you

Think of me lady, think of me at night
Think of me lady, I'll be alright

Lady so fair, lady so true
Are you in love, in love with me too
Are your dreams filled with love of me too

Lady so fair, lady so blue

Wish I was there loving you

Wish I was there loving you

Wish I was there loving you

Loving you

Loving you

Conant B. Rose © 1973

SHE MET ME IN THE STREET

I went down to the corner store
Getting myself something to eat
I should have known what it was all about
She met me in the street

I stopped my car and I peeked out
And man don't you know
She grabbed my collar - and said - man you jive
She punched me in the nose
I should have known what it was all about
She met me in the street

I rolled up my window - I was tired of this broad
My mind clicked - and - my foot slipped
She kicked in my door
I hunched down in my seat - and grabbed my piece man
I should have known what it was all about when
She met me in the street

My car wouldn't start - and she yelled some nasty things
I cried out baby, I love you
Don't you know, It's me

She stepped back from the door
And said some more
I jumped up from my seat - and - into the street
And banged her mind in the sewer, yeah

See, I blew her mind in the streets

Woo yeah

I should have known what it was all about

She met me in the street

Conant B. Rose © 1973

I JUST DON'T KNOW

Everybody wants to know which way I'm going
I don't know
Everybody wants to know which way my mind's flowing
I don't know
How can I know, when I don't know, what I'm doing here

Everybody seems to love my sorrows
How can I know about tomorrows
I don't know

I just seem to be swaying with my sorrows
I don't know
I just want to be there
Deep in all those, o yeah, my mind knows
I don't know

I may be afraid of loving someone else
Seem to be waiting alone
Felt all my days were gone, I just died,
I don't know
But I may be alive tomorrow
I don't know

I just got to learn to love my sorrows
I don't know
Maybe I'll be there
And oh
Maybe I won't tomorrow, y'all

Some things just never go right
But then
I just don't know
I just don't know
What's in sight
I just don't know
Conant B. Rose © 1973

HOLLYWOOD, CA, 1974

I JUST CAME FOR YOU

I just came out for you
Whew Lord, it's got to be me
When it's got to be me
You'll see
I just came for you

Don't you know I've done all this before
Can't you see I'm being me
Don't you know
I just came for you

When baby I've been trucking and ducking
Making tracks from many town and real
I've been moving and grooving
Getting down

I've been saving all my money and
I just got a dime
Now all I need is you baby
And we'll really do the town

When it's got to be me o yeah it's got to be me
There ain't no time for you to linger
Can't you see don't you know
I just came for you

Ya

I just came for you
Yeah baby
I just came for you
O ya

So you better get yourself up baby
And oh
Come with this singer
Come on baby
Don't you know
I just came for you
Conant B. Rose © 1974

IT WAS YOU AND ME

It was you and me
Well you're leaving me it's true
I can't go on without you
You were my world, my only dream
It was you and me
Forever you and me

Well you're walking out with him
What will I do without you
You were my world, my only dream
It was you and me

I never saw the tears
All through the years
I just wanted to believe you would always love me
Well now you're leaving me it's true
I can't go on without you

You were my world my only dream
It was you and me
Forever you and me

I wanted you to stay
I didn't want you to go away
I never saw the tears all through the years well,
Your walking out with him
What will I do without you

You were my world my only dream
It was you and me
O baby you and me
Yeah baby you and me
Conant B. Rose © 1974

*TONY ROSE AT RCA RECORDS, (A&R),
SUNSET BLVD., HOLLYWOOD, CA, 1974*

BACK ON TOP AGAIN

Back on top today
I said I'm on top to stay
Don't go away, just hear me say that baby
I'm back on top today
Hey

My old lady said she no go away
What can I say
Who baby hey
Just that I'm back on top again
I think I'll buy some gin

I just wanted to be cool
I didn't really want to use you
What can I do

Whoo lord I'm back on top again
Back on top again and
I still got plenty of friends

Heard tell the other day
My baby she no go away
She wanted to believe I was gonna be me
Oh lord did she say that
My baby moaned a song

Oh

I'm back on top again
Back on top again
Just hear me say
I'm back on top again
Conant B. Rose © 1974

I GET MY LOVIN DOWNTOWN

I get my Lovin downtown
I got my Lovin downtown
Just off seventh street
Down by the movie queen's house
She really wasn't home
Just used her phone
And dreamed my heart out with Miss Ding

I got busted in town down by the music center
Listening to all them coloured boys play
Had a good time
Joined in all the parades

Lucky for me it was just celebrating
For now
I'm going away
I found my new love in a box
She was a social fox

Crammed my body within hers
Who baby it was so much fun, it was gay
But then
I blew her away

I fixed my head in a twirl and
Watched the wind swirl
Just got down off an airplane

Fell out in the sky
When I was high
And was sucked by to earth
Down by main

I woke up one dark morning, down by the San Diego zoo
Tried to steal the elephant food
Oh lord, it was dead
Oh lord,

They just did it again

Said, let's get it on and do it, hey
Let's get it on and do it again
Said, let's get it on and do it
Let's get it on and do some sin

Who baby I said, I get my lovin downtown
Sunshine on my mind
I didn't know all those things
Oh baby I must be in heaven
Oh seems like I'm in heaven
It just seems like I'm here to stay gay

Jesus knows, I woke up last morning
Heated and all those things
My lord, I waited till seven
But then I found out fast
And before I knew it

My heart leaped uptown and then I knew
I was in heaven

Oh sweet heaven, sweet, sweet, heaven
My mind dreams of you lovingly
But for now, I get my lovin downtown
Conant B. Rose © 1974

**ONE OF THE HOLLYWOOD BANDS I BOOKED,
PRODUCED AND WROTE FOR, 1974**

ROBIN

Soon one day in the month of May
I'll be here waiting for you
And the robins, they will sing
Forever and ever, forever and ever

Late one day on a Milky Way
Our love will come once more
And the people then will say
Forever and ever, forever and ever

Touch your heart, whisper a sweet part
And you'll know what love can be
And we'll live in harmony
Forever and ever, forever and ever, forever and ever

You will be a surreal deity
And a vision I will be
And we'll be so very happy
Living in harmony
Forever and ever, forever and ever

Shining on in the west of here
In a world beyond belief
And we know that it won't be
Forever and ever, forever and ever

Soon one day in the month of spring
I'll be here waiting for you
And the robins, they will sing
Forever and ever, forever and ever

Shining on in the west of here
In a world beyond belief
And we know that it won't be
And we know that it won't be
Forever and ever, forever and ever
It won't be, forever and ever

Take your hand, fly away again
And at last you will be free
And the Robin sings to me
Forever and ever
A robin sings to me, forever
Conant B. Rose © 1974

YOU AIN'T GOING NOWHERE

You made yourself a promise
That you'd never go away
Cause you had yourself a lover
And felt he was bound to stay

You gathered up your dreams
And put them gallantly aside
Seems a week ago tomorrow
That you caught him in a lie
And you know that you ain't going nowhere

Ladies never ask a question
Seems you never did
Cause he'd kiss you in the morning
And lay with you in bed

It seems you had a way with men
You would put them in their place
And this man has gone and left you
With a belly full of aches

And you know that you ain't going nowhere.
You just get on back girl
Take the double track girl
You just keep on pushing
No time to be losing
You just get on up now
And close the door

Sometimes when you awake
You think of love
And then pretend
It's only something there
You can't explain
That binds you to the scene

You get the feeling
That it's something that you did
Something you said in a dream
And then you look around your bed
And you know that you ain't
Going nowhere

You just get on back girl
Take the double track girl
You just keep on pushing
No time to be losing
You just get on up now
And close the door

Conant B. Rose © 1974

TONY ROSE, LIVIN OFF SUNSET BLVD AND GOWER ST. 1974

MARS AND SPACE MAMA

I'm from Mars, man
I come from stars, man
I've got a space Cadillac,
I got a love that's out of sight.

I'm from Mars, man,
I come from stars, man.
I got a space mama with me,
We Rockin, Rollin, through the dip.

Makin love light years away, it's a Rockin Roll, Freakout.
Moondoggin on the Milky Way.
Dancin, Dancin to the beat, Dancin, Dancin with our feet,
Dancin, Dancin, floating on air, it's a Rockin Roll, Spaceout.

I'm from Mars, man
I come from stars, man.
I've got a space Cadillac,
I got a love that's out of sight.

I'm from Mars, man,
I come from stars, man.
I got a space mama with me,
We Rockin Rollin through the dip

Makin love light years away, it's a Rockin Roll, Freakout.
Moondoggin on the Milky Way.
Dancin, Dancin, to the beat, Dancin, Dancin, with our feet,
Dancin, Dancin, floating on air, it's a Rockin Roll, spaceout.

I'm from Mars, man
I come from stars, man
I'm from Mars, man
I come from stars, man
I'm from Mars, man
I come from stars, man
I'm from Mars, man
I come from stars, man
I'm from Mars, man
I'm from Mars, man
I'm from Mars, man
I'm from Mars, man
I'm from Mars, man
I'm from Mars, man
I'm from Mars, man
Conant B. Rose ©1974

GOOD BYE

Good bye, to a hard hearted woman like you
I'm glad to see that now we're through
These two years I've been with you
It's time I left this June

And it's too bad, too soon,
I'm glad I left this June,
Just like a winter moon
Like a summer tune,
And I know I won't be home soon

Please excuse my unconcerned way
I know that you wanted me to stay
I know the talk, what they'll say
It's just that I've got to go away

And everybody knows the wrong you've done
They've seen what these years have brung
I know just what I've done
I still take back all those songs I've sung

And it's too bad, too soon,
I'm glad I left this June,
Just like a winter moon
Like a summer tune,
And I know I won't be home soon

It's hard to say goodbye, my life
I'll try not to remember you at night
But I've got to go, make this flight
Might say I might cry, I guess it's alright

And it's too bad, too soon,
I'm glad I left this June,
Just like a winter moon
Like a summer tune,
And I know I won't be home soon

In your own way it's been nice knowing you
Seems like though I've always been the fool
It's time I left this June
Don't look for me real soon
And it's too bad, too soon for me to say
But I'm glad I left this June
Conant B. Rose © 1974

YOUNGER DAYS

In her younger days
She might as well been free
And if she ever finds out
I'm gonna head south

In her younger days
She might as well been free
Or headed out to sea
And if she ever sees God
I'm heading towards that fog

Searching for tomorrows and
Finding yesterdays
Always seeing someone like me again
Like me again
Like me again

In her younger days
She might as well been free
Or been just like me
And if she ever gets out
I'm staying south

In her younger days
She might as well been free
Swaying in the breeze
And if she ever comes down
I won't be around

Looking for yesterdays and
Finding tomorrows
Always seeing someone like me again
Like me again
Like me

In her younger days
She might as well been free
Or built a castle in quadrofidelity
And if she ever sees Jimi Hendrix
A true love she'll be

And if I ever move away from here
It's gonna take me a lot of years
And if I ever get away from this place
To find myself someone who cares
Maybe I'll go back there
And if she ever sees me gone
It's gonna take a lot to explain
And if she ever sees me gone
She'll forget my name

In her younger days
She might as well been free
Or been just like me
And if she ever finds out
I'm gonna head south

Searching for tomorrows and
Finding yesterdays
Always seeing someone like me again
Like me again
Like me again
Like me
Like me
Like me
Like me again

And if I ever move away from here
It's gonna take me a lot of years
And if I ever get away from this place
To find myself someone who cares

Maybe I'll go back there
Maybe I'll go back there
I guess I'll go back there
Maybe someday

In her younger days
She might as well been free
Or headed out to sea
And if she ever sees God
I'm heading towards that fog

Searching for tomorrows and

Finding yesterdays

Always seeing someone like me again

Yeah, always seeing someone like me again

Ya like me again

Like me again

Like me again

Like me

Ya like me

Like me again

Conant B. Rose © 1974

**TONY ROSE SIGNING AN ACT AT RCA RECORDS,
SUNSET BLVD., HOLLYWOOD, CA, 1974**

AN OCCASIONAL LOVE

I recall how we met
In the bottom of the pit
O' it was an occasional love
Something between us two
Something set

And we'd sleep holding tight
Our love holding tight
In the corner of our room
And we'd talk about love with our minds

And our sweet love would sigh
Beneath the sheets, O My!
And in our soft sweet love, the pillows would fly
Something in her eyes

I recall what we said
While lying next to her
And the dreams we dreamed in our minds
Something of a rebirth

And we'd wake making love
In the corner of our bed
Our love laughing and playing forever
Nothing more was said
And then one day, we'd love not ever again

I recall that love
And from my experience
I just knew that it would be forever
Something in her eyes

O, an occasional love
O, an occasional love
O, an occasional love
Conant B. Rose © 1974

A REAL SUPER FREAK

She's a real, real, super freak,
And her hearts a mellow beat
And she just really knows that she knows how to get down
She makes more sense than many
And anyone can get any
If they just get there on time.

She moves with all the in tunes
And knows all the who doos, yeah
And is a woman of her times
She's a non-discriminating, extra – xtra - rating
And she really knows how to stick it in the air

She's got a big double feature and a
Too bad greaser
And uh,
A feeling that you might have been there

A time of misinterpretation
And a feel for orchestration
She's everybody's feel
And for some their daily meal

Her name is everybody's mother, yeah
So deal with her you freakers,
She's all you want, more than you need,
And more than you can handle

She's your mother, yeah
Right off the streets
She's your sister, yeah
Gotten herself some meat

She's your old lady, yeah
Moving with the beat
She's just a real super freak
Freaking with the freaks,
And she really knows how to do it to you good

She moves with the glitter crowd
Caught up in their rhinestone jeans
She's a freak for a sandwich
And she loves being in between, yeah

Come on get on down with me
Come on get on down, she screams
To all the screamers
And her mouth waters hungrily
For a cat named C.B. Stinger

Now she moves it all around
And she really gets it down
And everybody knows she's a plaything
And when C.B. Stinger did it to her
She was just plain his thing

She's a too much mama
In her hip huggin gunners
And she really knows how to move her thing

She high steps to the beat
And gets down with Miss Ding
And the screamers really rave
They talk about her and C.B.
And the way they really drag

She moves with the glitter crowd
Caught up in rhinestone jeans
And she's a freak for a sandwich
She loves being in between
She's a too high mama caught up in her scene
And even though
Yeah, she still gets down with Miss Din
Conant B. Rose © 1974

THE FIRST BAND I MANAGED, PRODUCED AND SIGNED TO RCA RECORDS, LOS ANGELES, CA 1975

CAN YOU FEEL IT

Tired of being all alone

Too much for one person to do

Can't you feel the love that I have

You say that you don't, but you do

Can you feel it

Can't you feel it

Can you feel it?

Can't you feel it, I know that you do

Can you feel it, I know that you do

Can you feel it?

Koo Koo Ka Choo
Koo Koo Ka Choo

Koo Koo Ka Choo
Koo Koo Ka Choo
Conant B. Rose (C) 1975

YES I KNOW

You say it's not real
Just forget
Let time be your friend
I know it's not easy

When love has gone
And you find that
You can't go on
I know it's not easy

Yes I know
That you're leaving me girl
Yes I know
I can't fake it too much

You and I
We must reach for the sky
If we can
Just give it a try

Give it one more chance

Yes I know
Yes I Know
Conant B. Rose (C) 1975

SPACE FREAK

I want you to be
My rock and roll
Space freak baby
I want you to be
My lady
I want you to be
My rock and roll
Space freak baby
I want you to
Be my lady
Dance with me lady
Dance with me baby
Flying across space
It's a nice place
I want you to fly across
Space with me baby
I want you to be high
With me lady
I want you to fly
With me baby
I want you to be high
With me lady
Conant B. Rose (C) 1976

I'D RUN ACROSS THE SKY FOR YOU

I'd run across the sky for you, oh baby
I'd run across the sky for you, oh baby, yeah
I'd run across the skies, yes I would, oh baby, yeah, yeah
For you, for you, for you, for you, for you, all for you, for you, just for you, for you, you

St. Peter let me into heaven, oh yeah, yes he did now
St. Peter let me into heaven, yes he did, oh baby, yeah
St. Peter let me into heaven, Oh yeah, yes he did now, oh baby, yeah
And I know, I know, and I know,
I know, yes, I know, I know, I know

I'd run across the sky for you, yes, I would for you, oh baby
I'd run across the sky for you, oh baby, yeah, yeah, yeah, yeah
I'd run across the sky, yes I would, oh baby, yeah, yeah
And you'd know, ooooo, you'd know, you'd know, oh, you'd know

I'd climb the highest mountains for you, yes I would baby
I'd get in my spaceship and ride, for you, yes I would baby
I'd fly light years away, oh baby
I'd fly to the highest stars for you, oh baby
And you'd know, you'd know, oh you'd know, you'd know

I'd fly the highest mountains, I'd fly the deepest seas
I'd fly the highest stars, across the universe
Jupiter would not mean a thing
I'd fly, I'd flyyyyyyyyyyyyyyy

I'd fight the awesome wars, I know that I could with you
With my spaceship, and I couldn't be shot down, and you'd know, yes you'd know
You'd know, ooooo, you'd know, you'd know, oh, you'd know,
You'd know, ooooo, you'd know, you'd know, oh, you'd know

I'd fly across the skies, for you, yes I would baby
I'd run across the sky for you, oh baby
I'd run across the sky for you, oh baby, yeah
I'd run across the sky, yes I would, oh baby, yeah, yeah
For you, for you, for you, for you, for you, all for you, for you, just for you, for you, you

I'd climb to the highest stars, yes I would baby
I'd run across the furthest stars for you, oh baby
I'd run across the sky for you, oh baby

And you'd know, oh you'd know, you'd know,
You'd know, ooooo, you'd know, you'd know, oh, you'd know,
You'd know, ooooo, you'd know, you'd know,
oh, you'd know, that

I love you
Conant B. Rose © 1976

SPACE MUSIC FOR YOUR MIND

There's a place somewhere far above
Where my soul can ease all its troubles away
There's a place somewhere far above, where we can play

There's a place somewhere far above
Where my soul can take you to a higher place
Come with me lady, we'll play

I want to take you to a serious place
I want to take you to a higher space
Come girl, come with me, get higher

There's a place somewhere far above
Where my soul can ease all its troubles away
There's a place somewhere high above
It makes my spirit sway

There's a space somewhere far above
I want to take you to a serious place, yeah
I want to take you to a higher plane ooooooooooooo
I'll make sure your hearts on fire
Come girl, come with me, let's get higher

Space music for your mind
Space music for your mind
Space music for your mind
Space music for your funky mind, yeah, ummmmmmm

There's a place somewhere far above
Where my soul can ease all its troubles away
There's a place somewhere high above
Come with me girl, we'll play

There's a place somewhere far above
Oooooo, it makes my spirit sway
Come with me baby, we'll play

I want to take you to a mysterious place
I want to take you to a higher place
I'll make sure your hearts on fire
Come girl, come with me girl, let's get higher

Space music for your mind
Space music for your mind
Space music for your mind
Space music for your funky mind, yeah, ummmmmmm

Dear lady, come with me
Dear lady, can't you see
That I'm your spaceman, spaceman
Spaceman, spaceman
And we'll play some

Space music for your mind
Space music for your mind
Space music for your mind

Space music for your funky mind, yeah, ummmmmmm
I want to take you to a mysterious place
I want to take you to a higher place
I'll make sure your hearts on fire
Come girl, come with me girl, let's get higher
Space music for your mind
Space music for your mind
Space music for your mind
Space music for your funky Sun Ra mind, yeah
Conant B. Rose © 1976

DELIVERANCE

As I sit all alone
Thinking about what I've done
To deserve the life
Always on the run

Can't stop to give any one
My real feelings
Just staying hard to handle
All my dealings

Stopped caring about
Everyone else
Just getting all I can
For myself

Cause self is the only one
Watching out for me
Learning straight from life
Is how I'll be
No one educating me

Who I am
Just learning from other
Families and friends
Never allowing anyone
To get too close

Until one day
I got too close
To the other side the side of death
I thought I was ready
To take my last breath
But now you see where I am

Coming straight and
Hard from within

Letting you know
To never give up
Cause living on is
The harder one

I'll never be weak
As I was
Carving up because
Times were rough

In life everything
Has its reasons
To what happens to
All Gods creations

Now you must believe
In your self
No matter what cards

You were dealt
Take it from me
Life is worth living
Even if to appreciate
What we're given
Conant B. Rose (C) 1976

TWO OF MY BABIES MOTHERS, ONE SON AND HIS FRIENDS, 1977

NEVERMORE

Nevermore will I sing you a song
Nevermore can I hope to pretend
Now and then, Nevermore that I love you

Nevermore will I give you a smile
You can be sure
That I'll always try to forget you
Nevermore that I love you

Please don't say you need
Someone to hold you
Please don't say you love
Cause I'll love you

Nevermore will I sing you a song,
Nevermore can I hope to pretend
Now and then
Nevermore that I love you
Conant B. Rose © 1976

IT'S MAGIC

When I look into your eyes
It's magic
When I sing a song
I'll ease your troubles away

When I'm making love with you
It's magic
Holding you close in my arms
Most every day

You're the one who fills my heart in every way
I'm the one who wants you by my side

I'll say
Every time I come inside you
It's magic

Hey girl! Do a little thing with your mind
And take a ride with me
Conant B. Rose © 1976

MOON BABY, MOON WOMAN

Let me
Make love to you
I want to make love
To you

I want to
Be your space man
Lady
I want you to be my
Moon woman, baby
Conant B. Rose (c) 1976

BE MY LOVER TONIGHT

If I had you for a lover,
Time would only pass in a million eons of pleasure.
Your moon would be my sun, girl, I'd take you to forever.
I'd give myself to you,
Lay beside you, I'd be your only one. Oh girl. Oo, Oo, Oo

Be my lover tonight, Oo, Oo, Oo.
Be my lover tonight, Oo, Oo, Oo.
Be my lover tonight.

If I had you for an hour, I'd slip the world away,
Undercover, we'd be the only ones.
I'd fill your love with me, girl, I'd take you to another sun.
I'd sweep the galaxy, for eternity, you'd be the only one.

Girl, I'd say.
Oo, Oo, Oo.
Be my lover tonight. You know I want you baby to. Oo, Oo, Oo
Be my lover tonight. You know 1 want you baby to. Oo, Oo, Oo,
Be my lover tonight. You know I want you baby to. Oo, Oo, Oo
Be my lover tonight. You know I want you baby to, Oo, Oo, Oo
Be my lover tonight. You know I want you baby to, Oo, Oo, Oo
Be my lover tonight. You know I want you baby to, Oo, Oo, Oo
Be my lover tonight. You know I want you baby to, Oo, Oo, Oo
Be my lover tonight. You know I want you baby to, Oo, Oo, Oo
Be my lover tonight. You know I want you baby to, Oo, Oo, Oo
Be my lover tonight. You know I want you baby to, Oo, Oo, Oo

Be my lover tonight. You know I want you baby to, Oo, Oo, Oo
Be my lover tonight. You know 1 want you baby to.

If I had you for a lover, time would only pass in a million eons of pleasure.
Your moon would be my sun, girl, I'd take you to forever.
I'd give myself to you, lay beside you, I'd be your only one.

Oh girl.
Oo, Oo, Oo
Be my lover tonight. You know I want you baby to. Oo, Oo, Oo
Be my lover tonight. You know 1 want you baby to. Oo, Oo, Oo,
Be my lover tonight. You know I want you baby to. Oo, Oo, Oo
Be my lover tonight. You know I want you baby to, Oo, Oo, Oo
Be my lover tonight. You know I want you baby to, Oo, Oo, Oo
Be my lover tonight. You know I want you baby to, Oo, Oo, Oo
Be my lover tonight. You know I want you baby to, Oo, Oo, Oo
Be my lover tonight. You know I want you baby to, Oo, Oo, Oo
Be my lover tonight. You know I want you baby to, Oo, Oo, Oo
Be my lover tonight. You know I want you baby to, Oo, Oo, Oo
Be my lover tonight. You know I want you baby to, Oo, Oo, Oo
Oo, Oo, Oo,
Be my lover tonight. You know I want you baby to. Oo, Oo, Oo
Be my lover tonight. You know 1 want you baby to. Oo, Oo, Oo,
Be my lover tonight. You know I want you baby to. Oo, Oo, Oo
Be my lover tonight. You know I want you baby to, Oo, Oo, Oo
Be my lover tonight. You know I want you baby to, Oo, Oo, Oo
Be my lover tonight. You know I want you baby to, Oo, Oo, Oo

Be my lover tonight. You know I want you baby to, Oo, Oo, Oo
Be my lover tonight. You know I want you baby to, Oo, Oo, Oo
Be my lover tonight. You know I want you baby to, Oo, Oo, Oo
Be my lover tonight. You know I want you baby to, Oo, Oo, Oo
Be my lover tonight. You know I want you baby to, Oo, Oo, Oo
Be my lover tonight. You know 1 want you baby to.
Conant B. Rose ©1977

IMAGINE ME

And oh boy, I love you
I'll never get enough of you
I need your love inside of me every day
I need to feel you, O touch me boy
Imagine me losing you and you losing me

Hold me baby, hold me
Hold me, hold me close, hold me
O hold me so close to your body

Imagine me here with you, imagine me
Imagine me, imagine me, imagine me

Just want to say I'll give all my love to you
I'm so happy being here with you.
Just want to say I love you. Give my whole world to you
I'm happy being here with you

Our love is so true
Our love is so true
Our love is so true
I'll always love you

Our love will always stay true.
Imagine me loving you and you loving me
Conant B. Rose © 1977

***TONY ROSE WITH THE BOSTON CONSERVATORY OF MUSIC
GIRL FROM THE SEVENTIES AND THE MOTHER OF ONE OF MY SONS***

LOVE

I can't see her
Is she really there
Can I feel what doesn't touch me
I can't grab on and hold tight

So I'll love only myself
Where she was born
Love and life was
And is a gift to me
Birth till death is
My gift back to her

I'll walk the path that
I hope she's taken
It's so dark only
I see myself as the light

When I make a turn
Sometimes I don't exit
Almost like a lost soul
With no give

Should I make my own way there
Or should I wait until
She opens my door

Hello is anyone there
I scream out loud
Hoping for an answer
To a hidden question
Then a voice inside says
I'm right here
I'm always here
I'll never leave you
She says I can only leave her
And I have

But I've returned and it shows
In my life I can't see
I answer yes I've learned to see
What's not in front of my eye

I've learned to feel what I cannot touch
Then I felt my heart get a little bigger
I felt my mind expand a little wider
Almost a feeling of getting closer to my beginning

Can I wait until this day to see her
I guess I've already made that decision
As my mind expands and my heart grows
I feel smarter than any book could ever teach me

My knowledge is planted in my mind and it grows
But who waters it is not the question anymore
I've been blessed just like everyone else

But I choose to see it, I choose to feel it

Is it because of my longing or my yearning

To give is to receive

What will I give

Would I give who I am is the question

My answer is I will give to

Who I was proud to be

Conant B. Rose (C) 1977

THE BOY

The boy came back
To the city
Where he
Was born
To boogie
And get down with the girls

He came back to Boston
And man let me tell you
He seriously got around
Conant B. Rose ©1978

TEASER

She's a real good teaser

Girl's a real good pleaser

She will take you down, boy

Make you her own clown, toy

Oh, Oh, teaser, teaser, teaser, teaser, teaser, teaser

Leave her alone, she'll never take you on,

Take you on

Teaser, teaser, teaser, Teaser, Teaser, leave her alone.

She's a real good teacher

Girl's a real good bleeder

She will take you down, boy

Make you her own clown, toy

Oh, oh, oh,

Oh, Oh, Teaser, teaser, teaser, teaser, teaser, teaser,
Leave her alone, don't let her take you on, take you on

take you on, no,

teaser, teaser, teaser, leave her alone
Conant B. Rose (C) 1978

THE CITY OF NEW ORLEANS

The city of New Orleans pats you on your backside

As you race against time to catch that bus

You're long overdue for some extra training

In the social mores of big city life

You've got nothing to lose, you lost it early

So, you're coming to New York City to pay your dues

Don't you know you're not,

You're not a bottom lady

You're not a bottom girl.
Conant B. Rose (C) 1978

WAKE UP

Baby now that you are closer to me
And each day the changes of love make me feel uncomplimentary.
I can't believe the way that you feel about me,
And it's a shame girl, a doggone shame, that your love isn't what it's supposed to be.

But now, I look into your eyes girl, and I see the morning light, oooo
I look into your eyes girl, and I know its right.

Are you inviting me when the feeling is gone, lady.
I can't believe the things I feel, when you are gone away from me.
The feelings that I see in you, is something so majestic, oh girl,
You're like a dream come true in my heart, oo,
I can't believe the feeling is gone from you.

But, baby, take another look at love girl, I'll always be around,
And when you see, when you see me next time baby,
You'll know I ain't no clown.

Once your love was close to me,
When you're gone,
I can't believe the feeling, the feeling I used to know,
I know its gone girl, I know it's gone girl, can you tell.

I wake up every morning with some tear stains on my pillow, baby,
And your love lying there,
And it feels, oh it feels, feels so bad to me.

But, when you look around girl, and you see me coming near,
The feelings that I feel for you baby, aww, if the feeling is near,
0000, the feeling will be real, ooo,

So wake up baby, and try it once again.
When spring comes next year, I'm sure that we'll be together, ooo,
Together again, I know its crazy woman, oooo,
But I can feel it now, just you'll wake up one morning,
And then I won't be such a clown, such a clown, such a clown, ooooo,

But they'll be one day, oh I can tell, they'll be one bright sunny day,
Wake! I'll wake up in the morning girl, whoa,waoa,
And you'll be there, ooo, get down girl, you'll wake up,
I'll wake up, I'll wake up, I'll wake up, baby, yeah,
I'll wake up baby, you'll wake up, and soon,
Soon you'll be there.
Conant B. Rose ©1978

THE 1980'S

MY LOVE FOR YOU

My love for you is special
It's always on the one
And when you come around me
My heart beats, OO, so strong
Her love for you is untrue
It's not for you that's for sure
Check it out can't you see
I'm caring for you
Just remember boy

That my heart beats for you
And that I'll always be your friend

She makes promises
She can't keep
She'll tell you anything
That's a lie

My love for you is special
Jump to it now it's your chance

rap
You know I'm fine
And you know I'm sweet
So what are you waiting for
You got the best right here
It ain't over there

You better get with me
On the dance floor

Now I'm full of love
You can't cool me down
Keep moving with my beat
And I promise you
You'll be glad you did
Cause boy you know I'm sweet

Now all the boys want my address
But I'm saving it for you
Cause your slick fine, O boy, be mine
I'm waiting just for you

My love for you is special
It's always on the one
And when you come around me
My heart beats, OO, so strong
Conant B. Rose (c) 1981

FLATTER

She always flatters him
With love and poetry
She's always pleasing to the eye

But who is the one
But who makes the choice
And who makes the love survive

She's always kind to him
She makes him feel real good
Conant B. Rose (c) 1981

MY MUSE, YVONNE ROSE, AND ME, IN BERMUDA, 1981

SIMPLY HEAVEN (WEDDING SONG)

Together, forever my love, we will always be

Sharing, caring, our love in perfect harmony

You, you are simply heaven

You give me joy, the love I need

Oh, cause you, you are simply heaven

You give me joy in times of need

Darling, forever our love, till eternity

Our love will make it to the ends of the world

We'll raise a family

You, you are simply heaven

You give me joy the love I need

Oh, cause you, you are simply heaven

You give me joy, in times of need

So, if you believe in me
Like I believe in you

We'll stay together baby

There's nothing we can't do

You're all that I want

And all that I desire

Stay with me baby

And I'll take you higher

Stay with me baby

And I'll take you higher

Oh, Oh, together, forever, baby

We will always be

Sharing, caring, our love in certain harmony

Oh, cause you, you are simply heaven

You know girl, my dreams have been only about you

I'm so glad that our love has become one
I'm so glad girl, that you love me

Oh girl, our love is forever

Forever baby

You give me joy in times of need

You are simply heaven
Conant B. Rose © 1982

PEOPLE SINGING

People singing
People looking to the eastern skyway
There's a rumor
That will never go away
People singing for their lives
By, by, by, by,

There is a country
Full of marvelous wonders
People looking for
Their own thunder

People singing for their love
By, by, by, by,

People somehow know the world's in trouble
There's a danger of no tomorrow
People singing for their lives
By, by, by, by,

Now there's peace in the air
Carried by voices everywhere
I'm sure that this world
Will be, made up in God's family
Conant B. Rose (C) 1983

MY MUSE, YVONNE ROSE, AND ME, BOSTON MA, 1981

SHE'S THE GIRL

She's the girl of my every dream
She's the girl that makes me scream
She's the girl that I need so much
She's the girl that I love to touch

Every time I see that little baby
I go, Oh, oh, oh oh, oh oh, Oh oh
Every time that little girl drives me crazy
I go, Oh, oh, oh oh, oh oh, Oh oh

She's the girl of my every dream
She's the girl that makes me scream
She's the girl that I need so much
She's the girl that I love to touch

Every time I see that little baby
I go, Oh, oh, oh oh, oh oh, Oh oh
Every time that little girl drives me crazy
I go, Oh, oh, oh oh, oh oh, Oh oh

She's the Girl, ooooooooooooooooooo, yeah

She's the girl of my every dream
She's the girl that makes me scream
She's the girl that I need so much
She's the girl that I love to touch

Every time I see that little baby
I go, Oh, oh, oh oh, oh oh, Oh oh
Every time that little girl drives me crazy
I go, Oh, oh, oh oh, oh oh, Oh oh
Conant B. Rose ©1983

THIS GIRL

Time is something that is on my mind
Something that is understood
I've done a lot of dreaming in my time
Somethings I've thought I should have took

But you know this girl is on my mind
You know this little girl is hooked
It's alright, the feeling is right
It's alright, the feeling is right

Love and confusion is a deadly game
Something that is understood
I've had my share of women and some pain
Enough to write a book

But, you know this girl is on my mind
I can't get this sweet girl off my mind
You know this little girl is hooked
It's alright, the feeling is right
It's alright, the feeling is right

Time is something that is on my mind
Something that is understood
I've done a lot of dreaming in my time
Some things I've thought I should have took
But you know this girl is on my mind

You know this little girl is hooked
It's alright, the feeling is right
The feeling is right
It's alright

Love and confusion is a deadly game
Something that is understood
I've had my share of women and some pain
Enough to write a book

But, you know this girl is on my mind
I can't get this sweet girl off my mind
You know this little girl is hooked
It's alright, it's alright
The feeling is right
It's alright

Love and confusion is a deadly game
Something that is understood
I've had more than my share of women
And some pain
Conant B. Rose © 1983

ME WITH PRINCE CHARLES ALEXANDER (PRINCE CHARLES AND THE CITY BEAT BAND) AND MY AGENT OF TWELVE YEARS NEIL COOPER

THOSE LIES

When I see you
Walking with another
You say
Hey he's my brother
It don't matter

If it ain't the same guy
You look me in the face
And tell me those lies
Put on your brakes
And stop it girl
Conant B. Rose (C) 1983

TONY ROSE AND PRINCE CHARLES ALEXANDER OF PRINCE CHARLES AND THE CITY BEAT BAND, NEW YORK CITY, 1983

IN TIME

Mother gives her what she wants

In time

Father gives her what she needs

In time

She got everything a girl could want

She got her schoolbooks and she got her stash

She got everything she needs to have

In time

She's gonna be all mine, in time

In time, she's gonna be all mine, in time

Teacher say you'll be a star

In time

But, now you don't even know

Who you are.
Your gonna be all mine in time

I say to you, you got plenty of cash

You got your schoolbooks and you got your stash

You got everything you need to have

In time

I'm gonna make you mine

In time

In time

In time, I'm gonna make you all mine

In time
Conant B. Rose (C) 1983

RAINBOW (YVONNE'S SONG)

If you found a rainbow
Than you found a woman
You know

If you found a woman to love
The kind that takes you
High, high, above

If you found a rainbow
Then you found a lover
You know
Oh girl

If you found someone to adore
The kind who keeps you wanting for more
If you found a rainbow
Yeah you found a lover
000, you found a rainbow
Yeah you found a lover, 000 yeah, 000 yeah

How many lifetimes can you live
Without love in your heart
How many years can you survive
And not make love a part
I only know that my love for you
It grows and grows girl
And only you know

I only know I care for you
And girl I'll always be there
Cause girl you know my heart
Beats for you
Every moment of every day

You know girl
Every time I pass by your window
Every time I pass by your door
Girl you know
You're all I think about

Girl give me your love
Give me your touch girl, 0O0, Girl
Oh girl, my love's for you
It's for you girl
Only you

I only know my love is forever
It's forever, its forever girl
Forever girl

If you found a rainbow
Than you found a woman
You know

If someone is crazy about you
Let's all the world

Know her heart beats, beats for you
If you found a rainbow, yeah
You found a lover
OO, you found a rainbow
Yeah you found a rainbow
Conant B. Rose (c) 1983

MY MUSE, YVONNE ROSE, AND ME AT THE DURAN DURAN AND PRINCE CHARLES AND THE CITY BEAT BAND'S CONCERT AT MADISON SQUARE GARDEN, 1984

LET'S GET DOWN TONIGHT

We gonna party some more
Hey mama
This is just for you

Let's get down tonight
Let's go out tonight
And get the groove

Hey mama
This is just for you
We gonna dance and sing
We gonna do our thing

Hey mama
This is just for you
We gonna dance and party
Like we never did before
Is that right

Let's get down tonight
We gonna dance and party
Like you never did before
Is that right

We gonna do our thing
We gonna make you swing
Like you never did before
Conant B. Rose (C) 1983

TIME AFTER TIME

Time after time
I thought my love for you
Had eased on

I never thought of you
I never dreamed of you
Never wanted you

Time after time
I stopped my love
No one to cling too

I never wanted to
Never needed to

But then you came along
And brought back
All my loving feelings
My happy feelings are all back again

And then you came along
And gave my life a new meaning
And gave my life a happy ending

I'm in heaven when I'm touching you
Time after time
I walked the streets
My heart yearning

For the touch of you
The warmth of you
The Smell of you, baby

Time after time
I felt my heart growing colder
I never thought of you
Never dreamed of you
Never wanted to
Conant B. Rose (C) 1983

TONY ROSE IN THE STUDIO, RECORDING A PRINCE CHARLES AND THE CITY BEAT BAND ALBUM, PARIS, FRANCE - 1984

LOVES FOR REAL

Now that we have worked it out
I know that your loves for real without a doubt

I know that your loves for real
You have the perfect touch
You make my whole world
I want to shout

Girl you're what I need
Girl I'm existing for your love
I truly, truly, feel that
No one can ever take your place

I hope you know my loves for real
Now that we have worked it out,
I know that we can dance and shout
You have the perfect touch
And I know without a doubt this loves for real
Conant B. Rose © 1984

DON'T SAY GOODBYE GIRL

Don't say goodbye, girl
In my mind I understand the feelings
You've been going through
I've been going through them too

So girl please forgive me
Accept my love
I know sometimes you think
All of us guys are alike
So untrue

But there's one thing
I just want you to know
That my love girl
It, it's for you
My love girl it's for only you
Only you

In a little while
Your dreams will come true
In a little while
You'll forget sadness

In a little while
Your day will come through
They'll be no more sorrow, no more pain
Just gladness

Young girl
I've been watching you, watching you
I know all you've been going through
So, if you give me one more try
I'll do all I can do

So, don't tell, don't tell me, no
Don't tell me, don't tell me, no
Don't, don't, don't, say goodbye, girl

Please stay, oo, Ah
Please stay, oo, Ah
Please stay, oo, Ah
Please stay, oo, Ah

If you take a look around
You'll find the right answer
If you take one look around, find me
If you take a look around
I'm sure, I'm the answer

Please girl, look, look around
Hold me

Young girl
I've been watching you, watching you
I know what you've been through
So, if you give me one more try, one more try

I'll do all I can do
So don't, don't, don't, tell me no
Don't tell me no, don't tell me
Don't, don't, don't, say goodbye girl
Please stay, oo, Ah

Please stay, oo, Ah
Please stay, oo, Ah
Please stay, oo, Ah
Please stay
Please stay
Conant B. Rose © 1984

DISS REGARDING

Diss regarding all of those people
That said that they knew me when
I guess I'll always be in love
With them
I guess I always will

I'm diss regarding all of those people
Sometimes I think I'll never win
Sometimes I think I talk too much
At times I'm never still

But, oh, oh, oh, some people
They can see through me
And oh, oh, oh, I'll never be free

I'm diss regarding all of those people
The one's who threw rocks at me
I'll never fit in anyway
I'll never seem to please

I'm diss regarding all of those people
The one's she said would do me good
I think I'll fall in love again
I think I'll never be free

Sooner or later baby
You gonna find somebody crazy
Somebody crazy who loves only you

Sooner or later lady
You gonna find somebody crazy
Somebody crazy like me

Sooner or later girl
You gonna climb in my world
Sooner or later you gonna
Be mine
Conant B. Rose © 1985

TONY ROSE ON TOUR, GERMANY. 1985

YOU'RE NOT HERE

When the moon is clear, and the sun gone down
I can't sleep no more, cause you're not here

When the evening's done, and I'm all alone
I can't still my fears, cause you're not here
When the day's gone by, and the shadows fall
I can't stop my tears, cause you're not here

Oh I want to tell you
I'm still crazy about you girl
Oh my love girl, come on home
Oh I want to tell you, how much I care
I can't tell you baby, if you're gone

When the night falls, and the moon is clear
I can't still my fears, cause you're not here

Oh I want to tell you
I'm still crazy about you girl
Oh my love girl, come on home

Oh I want to tell you, how much I care
I can't tell you baby, if you're gone

When the moon is clear, and the sun gone down
I can't sleep know more, cause you're not here
When the evenings done, and I'm all alone
I can't still my fears, cause you're not here
Conant B. Rose © 1986

TONY ROSE, OUR EUROPEAN CONCERT PROMOTER, AND PRINCE CHARLES ALEXANDER OF PRINCE CHARLES AND THE CITY BEAT BAND IN THE STUDIO, NEW YORK CITY, 1986

LOST IN EGYPT

Sweet nothings
He whispers in my ears

Tells me lies
I don't want to hear

Playing with my feelings
Causing me to shed tears

I don't care
I'm not going to be his girl for long

There's always somebody
Somewhere who'll come, along

And take me away
From this horrible pain

Take me to a place
Where love never changes

Across the waters
Sun's, galaxies
I'll travel
Floating on a mist

He'll never find me
Destroy me

I'll get lost in Egypt.
China, Malaysia, Jupiter
It doesn't matter
Only worlds away
Will help end our lives

Distance - time machines
Shattered lives
Stained proof
On Saturn's rings
Conant B. Rose © 1986

MISSING YOU

I've been missing you
And your face against my neck

Missing you and the things
Our arms do

It's been time
To go away
The time's been spent
Missing you
And those places in our bed

Missing you
And the way you give your heart

Our loves a rainbow
In the mist of memories
A rainbow
The arc of our hearts

I've been missing you
I sure didn't mean to be
Missing you
But now I know
I can't stay away
It's alright I'm coming home
Cause I've been missing you

That's the story
Just to let you know
Our loves a rainbow
In the mist of memories
A rainbow
The arc of our hearts
Missing you
Conant B. Rose (C) 1987

YVONNE 'THE MUSE' ROSE (SOLID PLATINUM RECORDS), RON MOSLEY (RCA RECORDS), CECIL HOLMES (CBS RECORDS), TONY ROSE (SOLID PLATINUM RECORDS)

HEARTS OF LOVE

You may not find truth in life
And, some people tell you lies
But, I know there's a place for love
And I know some foolish, have hearts,
Hearts of love

And, sometimes there's a lonely time for life
And, some people grab you up, until you die
But, I know there's a place for love
And, I know some foolish, have hearts
Hearts of love

But, I know there's a place for love
And I know some foolish, have hearts
Hearts of love

But, I know there's a place for love
And I know some foolish, have hearts
Hearts of love

8ut, I know there's a place for love
And I know some foolish, have hearts
Hearts of love

You may not find truth in life
And, some people tell you lies
But, I know there's a place for love

And I know some foolish have hearts
Hearts of love
Hearts of love

But, I know there's a place for love
And 1 know some foolish, have hearts
Hearts of love

But, I know there's a place for love
And I know some foolish, have hearts
Hearts of love
Hearts of love, hearts of love, hearts of love, hearts of love,
Hearts of love, hearts of love, hearts of love, hearts of love

But, I know there's a place for love
And I know some foolish, have hearts
Hearts of love
Hearts of love, hearts of love, hearts of love, hearts of love,
Conant B. Rose © 1987

DEEP INSIDE YOUR LOVE

Deep in your love I will be
You're my emotion
Waiting for you
Uh ha, Uh Ha

Step inside
You will see
You're my desire

Deep in your love
Uh Ha Uh Ha
You'll find true love and romance
Waits for you

Softly kisses away, away
Deep in your love I will be
My emotion
Deep in your love
Uh ha uh ha

Sometimes I know that you're there
Waiting for my love
Deep inside
Uh ha uh ha

You'll find true love and sweet romance
With my love inside you girl

Sometimes you're so far away, far away
Somewhere inside of my dreams
I'll wait for your love
Deep inside
Uh ha uh ha

A kiss from your lips girl
Kiss from your lips girl

Softly we'll touch come closer
Your love is where I want to be

You're my emotion
Loving you away
Your love is where I will be

I'll take your charms
Deep inside of you
Uh ha uh ha, 000, Uh ha uh ha
Conant B. Rose © 1987

TONY ROSE, WITH HIS MUSE, YVONNE ROSE, RECORDING AT 'HIT CITY RECORDING STUDIO', NEW YORK CITY, NY 1987

BE MY LADY

Sweeter then the candy
You bring home at night
Girl I want to hold you
With all of my might

And as each day goes by
I thank my lucky stars
You're the girl of my dreams
The queen of my heart

So be my lady, oh yeah
Just be my lady, oh yeah
Well, be my lady, be my girl

Whenever we go out
You take my breath away
The guys they all see me
But, what can they say

You smile at me
And take my hand
We dance the night away
Closer and closer

I don't think that we could be friends
And not lovers
I know that I don't wanna live
With no other, girl
I don't think that we could be friends

And not lovers
I know that I don't wanna live
With no other, girl

Oh be my lady, be my girl
So, be my lady

The days they just go by
Our love just grows more and more
Together we can make it
Of this love I'm sure

We'll fill our hearts with love
And make it for always
We'll dance the nights away, closer and closer
Oh yeah, Oooo Yeah

I don't think that we could be friends
And not lovers
I know that I don't wanna live
With no other, girl

I don't think that we could be friends
And not lovers
I know that I don't wanna live
With no other, girl

Be My Lady, Be My Girl
So, Be My Lady, Be My Girl
Be My Lady
Conant B. Rose © 1987

TRUE LOVE

Deep in the heart of the jungle
Black eyed boy came up to me
Said let's go dancing at the palace
On 14th St.

He said love is what you need girl
Love is the answer

Down in the depths of the city
Crosstown on East 43d St.
There ain't nobody takin' pictures
Of our love
You know it's insane

He said love is what you need girl
Love is the answer
He's my true love

Upstairs in the back of the palace
He kisses me passionately
Our love is automatic
Everyone can see

Love is the answer
He's my true love
Conant B. Rose © 1987

TONY ROSE IN PARIS BACKSTAGE ON TOUR WITH ALAN ARTOUD, A&R, VIRGIN RECORDS FRANCE, GERMAN GUY, A&R, VIRGIN RECORDS GERMANY AND PRINCE CHARLES ALEXANDER FROM PRINCE CHARLES AND THE CITY BEAT BAND

I MADE A PROMISE

I made a promise to always be there
I made a promise to my love
I told him that I wouldn't despair
I made a promise to my love

You know my love is so good to me
You know my love will never set me free
I never, ever, never, want to be free
I made a promise to my love
My love, my love, my love,
My love, my love, my love.

I made a promise to always be there
I made a promise to my love
I told him that I wouldn't ever disappear
I made a promise to my love

You know my love is so good to me
You know my love will never set me free
I never, ever, never, want to be free

I made a promise to my love
My love, my love, my love,
My love, my love, my love.

You're so sweet and you're so fine
And baby, I'm giving you all my time

FOREVER YOURS

I'll never leave you until the end
Cause baby your my one and only friend

You're so sweet and you're so fine
That's why I'm giving you all my time

I made a promise to always be there
I made a promise to my love
I told him that I wouldn't ever despair
I made a promise to my love
My love is so good to me
My love will never, ever, set me free
Conant B. Rose © 1987

CALL ME UP

If you ever see my baby
Just tell him to call me up
Just put his dime in the telephone
And I'll be there before it drops

Just call my name
And I'll come runnin' baby
Just call my name
And I'll come runnin' baby

If you ever see that lost boy
Just tell him that I'm all, all alone
I'm here waiting for him
I'm waiting by the telephone

Just call my name
I'll come runnin' baby
I'll come runnin' baby
Just call my name, yeah
And I'll come runnin' baby
I'll come runnin' baby

If my baby's there with you girl
Just tell him that I'm here all, all alone
And I'll be, sitting, waiting for him
Tell him to use the phone

Just call my name
And I'll come runnin' baby
I'll come runnin' baby
Just call my name, yeah
And I'll come runnin' baby
I'll come runnin' baby
I'll come runnin' baby

Just call my name
And I'll come runnin' baby
I'll come runnin' baby
Conant B. Rose © 1987

TONY ROSE, BOBBY BROWN AND MAURICE STARR, BOSTON, MA 1987

RAINBOW

I want to see the rainbow
When the rain goes away
Cause it fills my heart with love
And it takes away the pain

Tell me why, Oh why
Can't I get close, close enough to feel
Feel the colors
The rainbow may reveal

Should I try to find
The end of the rainbow
Where it's sad
A pot of gold may glow

Rainbow, Rainbow, Rainbow, Oh, Oh, Oh, rainbow
Rainbow colors shining bright, so bright
And rainbow you put the light in my life
I need you so, oh rainbow
How much you'll never know

Can't you see the tears
Falling down my face
Rainbow you dry them
And you never leave a trace

My heart is broke
As bad as things may seem
You fix me up
And fullfill all my dreams

I need someone, something
To call my own
Oh rainbow
Don't you ever go

Rainbow, Rainbow, Rainbow, Oh, Oh, Oh rainbow
Rainbow colors shining bright.
So bright
And rainbow you put the lite in my life
I need you so, Oh, rainbow

You paint my world with love
Rainbow I see you
Light up the sky
Behind the clouds
And you're in my eyes

I'm standing all alone
So rainbow don't you ever, ever go
Rainbow, Rainbow, Rainbow, Oh, Oh, Oh
Conant B. Rose (C) 1987

NEVER

You will know I'll travel one day far away
And you will be so sad
But nothing can stop me to go from you
As our love is finished

There is no way to stay
But only to have another life
What will you do then, don't be sorry
Start another life
Don't stay alone
I won't come back
So don't wait for me
I have a new life that begins now

Be strong in your new life
And don't think too much
You will have your life
Which might be lovely
So don't worry
For you will smile again also

In your new heaven
That night will start soon
I want to stay free without you
don't hope for me to come back to you

Never, Never, Never, Never
Now I feel inside good
Every day I got sun
Because I am happy

To discover again a new life
That I never knew before
Enjoy things that life gives, and no one will stop me to do it
What will you do then
That might start soon

I want to stay free without you
Don't hope me to come back to you
Never, Never, Never, Never
Conant B. Rose (C) 1987

I NEED YOU

I need you now in my heart
As my deep feeling is so strange
That I can prove by my love
I can tell you that my love will never change

Every ten years will pass by
I'll stay the same
You can trust me
That no one can take your place

Even when you are away
My love is strong
No one can give me
So much hot and burning sensation
As you give me

So don't worry
I feel sad tonight
That you are not here
How much I miss you
When you are away

I feel so lost
My hope is to have you
Back in my heart
So come back soon

I am waiting for you

I am burning

Conant B. Rose (C) 1987

TONY ROSE, HIT CITY RECORDING STUDIO, ROXBURY, (BOSTON) MA. 1988

SWEET LOVE

Every night I hope, and pray, yeah
Sweet love's gonna come my way, yeah
And every girl that passes me by
I say, sweet love you're gonna come my way

And every day my heart beats closer to you girl
In every way I feel your magic for me girl
In every way I want to feel you
And every day I want your love, that's right

And every morning
When my baby wakes
Sweet love's gonna come her way

And every day
When I'm rushing to class
I say, sweet love's gonna come my way
Conant B. Rose © 1988

TONY ROSE AND MAURICE STARR RECORDING A NEW KIDS ON THE BLOCK ALBUM AT TONY ROSE'S 'HIT CITY RECORDING STUDIO', ROXBURY (BOSTON) MA., 1989

LOVE'S A FACT

When we we're just in grade school
Our parents were the best of friends
They took us everywhere
Now that's a fact, that's a fact

Now we're always together
Through rain, stormy weather
Our love sees us through
Now that's a fact, love's a fact

Darling when you're here by my side
I feel so right
And baby when you're close to my body
You know we're tight

Now that's a fact, Love's a fact
Conant B. Rose (C) 1989

TONIGHT'S THE NIGHT

Girl you'll always be my baby, girl you and I
You'll be my number one love, baby, girl you and I
Girl you know we'll stay forever, until eternity
I'll be your number one love baby, girl you and I
I need no other love girl, baby, girl just you and I
Together we will make love baby
Girl you and I

I will take the rainbows, baby
And give them all to you
If you and I could stay forever, girl you and I

I'll be your number one love baby, girl you and I
I'll take no other hearts now baby, girl you and I
Together we can dream love baby
Together we can come, to be only one love baby
Girl you and I
Conant B. Rose (c) 1989

LONELY NIGHTS

A lonely night is, oh baby
A lonely night is
A lonely night is, oh so lonely

I can't spend another lonely night like this
I just can't spend this night
Waiting for things to be alright
I just can't spend another lonely night like this
The clock on the wall keeps talking
While the beat of my heart keeps walking
I just can't stand another night like this

A lonely night is, oh baby
A lonely night is
A lonely, lonely, lonely, night this is

I keep hearing the things you say
Although you're so far away
A lonely, lonely, lonely, night this is

Our last date you stood me up
But you're still my squeeze, buttercup
A lonely night this is, baby
I want you to know I'm fine
And our love is, oh so, divine

A lonely, lonely, lonely, night this is
A lonely night is, oh baby
A lonely night is
A lonely, lonely, lonely, night this is

At home I wait patiently
Just waiting for you to call me
A lonely, lonely, lonely, night this is

In the mirrors I see you there
But I know you just don't care
A lonely, lonely, night this is
A lonely night is, oh baby
A lonely night is
A lonely night is, oh so lonely

A lonely night is, oh baby
A lonely night is
A lonely night is, oh so lonely
Conant B. Rose © 1989

TONY ROSE

THE 1990'S

TONY ROSE, SUNSET - GOWER STUDIOS, HOLLYWOOD CA. 1995

NOVEMBER

She wore a cotton blend of tiger cages
Outrageous blue

So serene she had to squeeze
Her leaner and meaner
Than a chicken dog
Gone weird

She go now
Jumping over the moon
Landing where it's sandy
Where life's a beach

Not chocolate candy
Into a Ford
I held the door
I fall asleep

Drove all night
They played quiz songs
The early light opened our eyes
Chocolate white girl screaming
Someone she knew had died

Stand up
Straighten outside
By side together

The weather is goodness sakes
Forever

We be striving to stay alive
Until one hundred and five
Jiving with the best
In November

You're beautiful
Just us forever
In November
Conant B. Rose (C) 1990

STILL MISSING YOU

With a kiss she awakes me
I recover
Look how she makes me shake all over

Never imagine
I couldn't cope
Things never work out
Quite the way I hoped

Still missing you
Still wishing you
Still want you near
Still missing you
Still wishing you
Still hold you near

Now that you've taken
Control of me
This indiscretion
Forgive me please

Since our separation
I awake each day
Afraid by the dawn-light
You'll steal away

Still missing you
Still wishing that
You and I
Forever after

I fall apart
I take you to my heart
And every day I pray
That there will come a day
Still missing you
Conant B. Rose (C) 1990

WHISPERS

Let me think back to my younger days
As I look up to hear what the teachers say
Can't keep my mind on what's behind the doors
All I worry about is what life has in store

Being trapped in a world that I can't be myself
I keep hearing the voices say that boy he needs help
Another lost soul what a waste of life.
Just what a child needs to hear to give up the fight

Finally the doors open am I really freed
Can I go out in life and plant my own seed
To grow and grow off what I really know
To trust in my mind and the Creator of my soul

This was the pattern that my life was taken
I've come to realize those whispers were mistaken
I'm following my dreams in this path of life
With no guarantees for what is right

Just trusting in what I feel from deep down inside
Taken life straight on with nothing to hide
Knowing who I m and believing in the lord above
I finally let Him in now all I feel is love

It was sent to me in a dream by a dove
In a way only the lord could think of
I still hear the whispers but now they're saying
To get where he is what price is he paying

They don't understand that I paid my dues
Now I keep my head up with nothing to lose
Cause I was given strength from the lord above
A strength so hard its name is love

Now don't get me wrong I'm a survivor of life
I'll do what I have to do to finish my flight
No fear in my eyes cause I know what's coming
As my soul rises up with the absence of fear
The higher and higher I go the whispers disappear
Conant B. Rose (C) 1991

ME AND YVONNE 'THE MUSE' ROSE, NEW YORK CITY, TIMES SQUARE, 1993

A KISS GOODNIGHT

Girl you been on my mind
Since the day we met
You, got that certain touch
I can't forget

You're all of my hopes and dreams
My life's desire
You're the girl that I'm thinking about
Each and every night

And that's why girl my love for you grows deeper
With every day
And that's why girl my love for you
It's here where I want it to stay

Girl you been in my life
Sometime before
I can tell
Cause you got the kind of love
My heart beats for

And every day, my baby
That life goes by
I'll be there
To hold you, to squeeze you
And get
A kiss goodnight
Conant B. Rose (C) 1993

HEY GIRL

Hey girl, you got to find out
What it is girl, that is wrong with your mind
Hey girl, you got the number
Is it right

Hey girl you got the number
And I'm here right by your side
I know that we'll be together
All the time...right

Now listen girl
I'm gonna take you, I'm gonna tell you
Something baby that's on my mind. - yeah

I'm gonna rock you, I'm gonna tell you
Something... that you're mine all mine...yeah
Oh, yes girl
I'm gonna take you, girl, and make you feel alright. Right now

I'm gonna rock you girl with my affection
Oh girl, oh, What's on your mind yeah

Hey girl you got to find out
What girl is on your mind - yeah
Hey girl you got to find out
What girl is it on your mind - yeah

Come on girl talk to me baby
Tell me about it
Hey girl you got to find out
What girl is on your mind, mind

I love you girl all my affection
Cause girl you know
Your mine, all mine, all mine, all mine, all mine
Hey girl I want to do the right thing
Tell me, that I'll be alright

And hey girl, I'll love you forever
0, baby girl, it's alright
Listen girl listen

All my loving, and all my talking
I'll give you something that
Is really too right - right

I'm gonna rock you, I'm gonna talk you
I'm gonna tell you girl, and make you feel alright right
I'm gonna make you feel my affection
I got a love girl that is really too right
I'm gonna tell you something special
I'm gonna rock you

Give you girl my, my, my, high (morning, noon and night)
Hey girl you got the right thing
You're giving me what's on my mind. – yeah
Hey girl I'll love you forever
Conant B. Rose (C) 1994

KEEP RISING

People keep rising
People keep rising
People keep rising
Because they'll soon a come a tumbling, tumbling down
Because they'll soon a come a tumbling, tumbling down
Conant B. Rose (C) 1995

FACE OF LOVE

We can cross the barren desert
And not die of thirst
We can wander far in safety
And never lose our way

We can talk in a foreign place
And all will understand
We shall see the face of love
And live again

Don't be afraid
I'll walk before you always
Just follow me
We'll see the face of love
We can pass through raging waters
And not drown
We can walk through burning flames
And not be harmed

We can stand before the power of hell
And death is at our side
We shall see the face of love
And live again

We shall stand before the power of good
And God is at our side
And we shall see the face of our love

And live again.

And live again.

Conant B. Rose (c) 1995

**ME, AND MY MUSE, YVONNE ROSE, AT HOME,
IN LOS ANGELES, CHRISTMAS, 1995**

ANGEL

Across the darkened sky
I looked around I looked
And saw an angel

She looked at me I looked and saw
I saw an angel

Across the moon above
I closed my eyes
I looked and saw, I saw an angel
There she was looking at me
I saw the light
I saw an angel

I looked around I looked around
I looked and I, I saw an angel
I saw an angel Oh, Oh I, I saw an angel

When I was born
I saw a fire in the sky
I looked, I saw an angel
In my arms, I saw, I saw, I saw,
I saw, I saw, I saw, an angel

There she was looking at me
I saw my life, I saw an angel
I saw the light
I saw the light
I saw an angel

She was
I saw an angel
I saw, I saw, an angel
I saw, I saw, I saw, an angel
There she was looking at me
Beckoning me
I saw an angel
1 saw an angel

Across the darkened stairways -
I walked into the house
I saw an angel
I saw, I saw, I saw, an angel

Into the crowded night I went
I looked up
And I saw an angel
There she was
Looking at me, beckoning me
I saw the light

I saw an angel
I saw the light
I saw the light
I saw an angel
Conant B. Rose © 1995

IN THE NIGHTS GLOW

The hours before I sleep
I pray to the lord
Above me
My soul to keep

And if I die
Before I wake
I pray to the lord
Above me
My soul to take

In the night glow
The night glow
Conant B. Rose (c) 1995

T & BJ

Dis is a story about a boy and girl
Who live in the projects
T & BJ hooray

Times were hard for dem
And they was tryin to be friends
Eatin in the hallway
When they was only ten

KJ was in fact lookin to Rac attack Jac
On BJ's ass.
The boys knew that was down
Behind the back attack door
On the third floor

Niggers was every where
Talkin bout this, Talkin bout that
But everybody knew
It was time to check on BJ's little skinny ass

T & BJ was up on the tenth floor
Playing silly shit
Like little kids
Runnin uptown, Runn downtown
Runnin through the halls
Makin lots of noise and sounds

No elevator was runnin
No elevator was runnin
So I can tell I'm what's up
I don't know where to find them
I start lookin

But KJ's boys Rac attack my jaw
Niggers was hungry lookin for BJ's ass
Made me tell em what floor they was on
Life in heaven ain't easy
chorus
Just wanna hold you tight
All day, all night
Just wanna hold you tight
All day, all night
Conant B. Rose (C) 1996

ACROSS THE DESERT

You and I could be as one
Across the desert
We'll travel across the Sun
Across the desert

We'll make the pyramids our home
Across the desert
Our hearts will beat as one
Across the desert

Soon we'll be home
Across the desert
Across the desert
Conant B. Rose (C) 1996

I'LL BE THERE FOR YOU

When you're feeling down and alone
When there's no one else to turn to
When the world seems sad and so blue
I'll be there for you

If everyone has turned you away
If all the world has made you afraid
If all you need is a helping hand
Don't fear I'll be there

Just follow your dreams
Just follow your star
Boy you know who you are
I'll be there

Just call out my name
Don't you be afraid
Just call out my name
I'll be there

When the door to life has been shut
And there's no one else to talk to
When all is sad and alone
When the nights through
I'll be there for you

When there's no one to come home to
And every day you say it's not true
Even when you still have some doubts
Don't fear I'll be there

Listen boy
I know you think sometimes
Life has put you down
And there's nowhere to turn
No one to talk to

I know your heart's been broken
Too many times
But understand I'm here for you
I just want you to know

Just call out my name
Don't you be afraid
Just call out my name
I'll be there for you

If everyone has turned you away
If all the world has made you afraid
If all you need is a helping hand
Don't fear I'll be there

Just call out my name
Don't you be afraid
Just call out my name
I'll be there for you
Conant B. Rose (C) 1996

JESUS

Do you care about Jesus
Do you care about Love
Do you care about feelings deep inside

Do you care about people
Do you care about right or wrong
Do you care about the way in which you live

Do you care about Jesus
Do you care about the one above
Do you care about a thing called love

Well I know a place where it's warm inside
And I know a. place where it's free
And I know a place where the eagles fly
We'll be safe there just you and me
Conant B. Rose (C) 1997

IN NEED OF YOUR LOVE

Girl it's been a long time and I've
I mean me watching you
And every time I see you
I want to tell you how I feel

I hope you can understand why
I haven't said anything until now
But I think it's about time
I let you know
I'm in need of your love

And girl when I'm feeling lonely
Sad and blue
I just remind myself
How much I love you

And if we should ever.
Get together
You will see
That this love is
Just for you

Baby I was really quite surprised, ah
When you said that you loved me too
But you haven't begun to realize
The strength of our love and ecstasy
In need of your love

I've got to hold you tonight, girl
I want your love
Cause it makes me feel so right

In need of your love
Girl I'm thinking of you
Each and every day

And when I need you
I call out your name
Only to hold you close
And squeeze you tight

Your touch would complete
This heavenly night
You're the lady of my life

Your my lady I have you all deep inside and
I'm in need of you in my heart
Cause I've got you in my mind

In need of your love
I've got to hold you tonight girl
I want your love
Cause it makes me feel so alright
In need of your love
Conant B. Rose (C) 1997

FLY WITH ME

Fly with me, to all the old places, where we used to go to.
Can't you see, I would always want to be with you.

I want to fly.
I want to fly away with you, I wanna.
I want to fly, I want to fly away with you,
I want to fly.

Fly with me, to all the old places, where we used to run to.
Can't you see I would always, want to be with you.

I want to fly.
I want to fly away with you, I wanna.
i want to fly, I want to fly away with you,
I want to fly.

Fly with me, to the tall standing places,
Where our love was so free.
Can't you see I would always want to be with you.
Fly with me, to all the old places,
Where we used to run to.
Can't you see I would always want to be with you.

I want to fly.
I want to fly away with you, I wanna.
I want to fly, I want to fly away with you.
I want to fly

I want to fly, I want to fly,
I want to fly away with you I wanna.
I want to fly, I want to fly,
I want to fly away with you, I wanna fly.

Fly with me, to the city, of New York City.
Can't you see,
I would always want to be around you.

Fly with me, to all the old places, where we used to go to.
Can't you see,
I would always want to be with you.

I want to fly, want to fly,
I want to fly away with you, I wanna.
I want to fly, I want to fly,
I want to fly away with you
I wanna.

I want to fly, I want to fly,
Want to fly away with you I wanna.
I want to fly, I want to fly,
Want to fly away with you

I wanna.
Want to fly. I want to fly,
I want to fly away with you, I want to fly.
Conant B. Rose © 1999

I TOOK THE RISK

Did you ever find yourself cross the path of no return
Did you ever see yourself take the road and then you burn
But I took the risk, I paid the dues, I took the stand
I could have fought it, instead I choose

But I took the risk, I paid the dues, I took the stand
I could have fought it
Instead I choose.

Did you ever say to yourself, I can do it
And then you win
Like a bat out of hell, you run right to it
And then you take a stand

But I took the risk, I paid the dues, I took the stand
I could have fought it
Instead I choose.
I took the risk, I paid the dues, I took the stand
I could have fought it, instead I choose

But I took the risk, I paid the dues, I took the stand
I could have fought it
Instead I choose.
I took the risk
I paid the dues
Conant B. Rose © 1999

TONY ROSE

THE 2000'S

TONY ROSE, PUBLISHER/CEO
AMBER COMMUNICATIONS GROUP, INC., 2000

SOMETIMES IT'S TRUE

Sometimes it's true
Sometimes it's true
Sometimes it's true, that I'm a sad boy
That I'm a sad boy
That I'm a sad boy
That I'm a sad boy

Sometimes it's true
Sometimes it's true
Sometimes it's true, that I'm a bad boy
That I'm a bad boy
That I'm a bad boy
That I'm a bad boy

If you had known me
If you had shown me
If you had given me love
If you had shown me the way

Sometimes it's true
Sometimes it's true
Sometimes it's true, that I'm a sad boy
That I'm a sad boy
That I'm a sad boy
That I'm a sad boy

If you had known me
If you had shown me
If you had given me love
If you had shown me the way

Sometimes it's true
Sometimes it's true
Sometimes it's true, that I'm a sad boy
That I'm a sad boy
That I'm a sad boy
That I'm a sad boy

Sometimes it's true
Sometimes it's true
Sometimes it's true, that I'm a bad boy
That I'm a bad boy
That I'm a bad boy
That I'm a bad boy

If you had known me
If you had shown me
If you had given me love
If you had shown me the way

If you had known me
If you had shown me
If you had given me love
If you had shown me the way
Sometimes it's true
Conant B. Rose © 2000

IN THE MIDDLE OF THE NIGHT

In the middle of the night
I will always remember
You and I holding tight
You and I in love forever

In between we are making love
Sharing love forever
And then one day you went away
Taking away all my happiness
In the middle of the night
I will always remember
You and I holding tight
You and I in love forever

Will you take all that away from me
Will you take away my sorrow
Will you take away my everything
All the love you bring, tomorrow

In the middle of the night
I will always remember
You and I holding tight
You and I in love forever
Conant B. Rose © 2000

COMPLETED TWO BOOKS OF AN EIGHT BOOK DEAL WITH BOOK PUBLISHER, JOHN WILEY & SONS; YVONNE 'THE MUSE' ROSE, ASSOCIATE PUBLISHER, AMBER BOOKS; CAROL HALL, SENIOR VICE PRESIDENT, JOHN WILEY & SON'S; TONY ROSE, PUBLISHER, AMBER BOOKS. PHOENIX, AZ, 2000

DOWN BY THE SEASHORE

Laying with you, listening to the radio
Our feet in the sand.
Down by the seashore.

It's the fourth of July.
The red, white and blue.
Everybody's here.
Down by the seashore.

Don't know if I'm ever gonna make it through.
Don't know if I'm ever gonna see you again.
Don't know if I'm ever gonna make it through.
Don't know if I'm ever gonna see you again.

It's a wonderful morning, wishing you were here to say.
Turn up this song, baby. It's beautiful.
Down by the seashore.

Still thinking of you, though I'm with somebody new.
We'll always be here together.
Down by the seashore.

And, I don't know if
I'm ever gonna make it through.
And, I don't know if
I'm ever gonna see you again.

And, I don't know if
I'm ever gonna make it through.
And, I don't know if
I'm ever gonna see you again.

If I'm ever gonna see her again.
If I'm ever gonna see her again.

And, I don't know if I'm ever gonna make it through.
And, I don't know if I'm ever gonna see you again.
And, I dont know if I'm ever gonna make it through
And, I don't know If I'm ever gonna see you again.
If I'm ever gonna, see her again.
If I'm ever gonna, see her again.

It's a wonderful morning,
Wishing you were here to say.
Turn up this song, baby.
It's beautiful.
Down by the seashore.

Still thinking of you, though I'm with somebody new.
I'll always be here with you.
Down by the seashore.

And, I don't know, If I'm ever gonna see her again
And, I don't know, If I'm ever gonna see her again

Laying with you, listening to the radio,
Our feet in the sand.
Down by the seashore.

Down by the seashore.
Down by the seashore.
Down by the seashore.
Down by the seashore.
Down by the seashore.
Conant B. Rose © 2001

**TONY ROSE, PUBLISHER, AMBER/COLOSSUS BOOKS;
HAKI MADHUBUTI, PUBLISHER, THIRD WORLD PRESS;
MAX RODRIGUEZ, HARLEM BOOK FAIR;
KASSAHUN CHECOLE, AFRICA WORLD PRESS/ RED SEA PRESS;
W. PAUL COATES, PUBLISHER, BLACK CLASSIC PRESS, 2002**

BIG BOOTIES

I like the beach and those big booties on em, oh man
I like em, I like em, I need em
I like them tall girls with the big booties on fire
I like em, I like skinny girls with those big booties!

I like them California girls
It's true
Their booties swing
They're so big
I want to get with em

I like the beach, I like the beach
I like the beach with them big booties on em

I like, I like the beach
I like the beach
With them big booties on it
Conant B. Rose © 2002

ME, MY MUSE, ASSOCIATE PUBLISHER, YVONNE ROSE, BUSINESS PARTNER, SAMUEL P. PEABODY AND AMBER/COLOSSUS BOOKS AUTHORS, 2002

THE OPENING OF THE FIRST AFRICAN AMERICAN PAVILION AT BOOKEXPO AMERICA, TONY ROSE, AMBER BOOKS, FOUNDER AND EXECUTIVE DIRECTOR; BILL COX, PUBLISHER, BLACK ISSUES BOOK REVIEW; NIANI COLOM, GENISSIS PRESS, FOUNDER; ADRIENNE INGRAM, FOUNDER. 2004

THE 2010'S

TONY ROSE, NAACP IMAGE AWARD
WINNER FOR OUTSTANDING LITERATURE

BABY

Baby, oh, oh, baby
Baby, oh, oh, baby
Baby, oh, oh, baby
Baby, oh, oh, baby.

I love that boy so much
I love that boy it's true
That's the boy for me
That's the boy that I want

He makes my heart so free
He makes me want him so bad
He makes me do everything
He makes my love come down

Every night I think of him
Every night I think of his love
Every night I think of him

Every night my heart goes
Bomp, bomp, bomp
Bomp, bomp, bomp
Bomp, bomp, bomp

Baby, oh, oh, baby.
Baby, oh, oh, baby
Baby, oh, oh, baby
Baby, oh, oh, baby

He make my heart so free
He makes me want him so bad
He makes me do everything
He makes my love come down
Conant B. Rose (C) 2012

TONY AND YVONNE ROSE WITH SOME OF THEIR AMBER/COLOSSUS BOOKS TITLES 2012

LOVE IS

Love is beautiful, Love is giving, Love is sharing, Love is kissing, Love is French kisses, Love is helping, Love is unconditional, Love is bi-lateral, Love is everything, Love is what you need, Love is making sure, Love is without a doubt, Love is caring, Love is a gift, Love is what do you need, Love is you, Love is me, Love is gay, Love is straight, Love is bi-sexual, Love is pan-sexual, Love is up, Love is down, Love is crucial, Love is a man, Love is making Love, Love is mother, Love is father, Love is a child, Love is demanding, Love is overwhelming, Love is being thankful, Love is Lovely, Love is good, Love is being humble, Love is necessary, Love is a baby, Love is satisfying, Love is a hug, Love is holding, Love is a touch, Love is a joint, Love is a girl, Love is a boy, Love is a woman, Love is insatiable, Love is always, love is never, Love is being, Love is all you need, Love is connecting, Love is knowing, Love is wrong, Love is right, Love is selfish, Love is strong, Love is courage, Love is strength, Love is good, Love is bad, Love is sex, Love is lust, Love is jealous, Love is sexy, Love is magnificent, Love is loving, Love is family, Love is marriage, Love is a partner, Love is a boyfriend, Love is a girlfriend, Love is you, you are Love, Love is who you are, Love is a song, Love is a flower, Love is a play, Love is a movie, Love is a book, Love is a poem, Love is touching, Love is her, Love is him, Love is needing.
Love is, as the Beatles said, **All You need!**
Conant B. Rose © 2016

I THINK I LOVE YOU
Jimi Hendrix © 1968

THE JOURNEY OF LIFE IS EVERYTHING

Conant B. Rose © 2016

TONY ROSE, FEBRUARY 2018

And now that I'm at the end of my time

Had some terrible illnesses, there was no cure, nowhere to run, nowhere to hide, baby

Please note that I had some serious fun and made some serious money

Doing what I loved, music and books, books and music and honeys

That's all I did, books, music, money and honey.

Thank you to the Lord above, for answering all of my prayers

By making sure I was able to help myself and help so many more,

Going places and doing things that little poor, project/newspaper boy, never knew he could.

From Roxbury (Boston) to Texas, Amarillo, Witchita Falls, Japan, Tokyo, Misawa, Hawaii, Honolulu, Korea, Vietnam, Thailand, Bangkok, San Francisco, Mexico, Boston, Chicago, St Louis, Cleveland, Los Angeles, San Francisco, Oakland, Boston, New York City, Bermuda, Cancun, Jamaica, St. Thomas, France, England, Nice', Rome, Milan, Marcella, Manchester, Liverpool, Scotland, Glasgow, London, Paris, Munich, Berlin, Belgium, Brussels, Madrid, Barcelona, England, France, Italy, Spain, Germany, Amsterdam, Rotterdam, Holland, Toronto, Montreal, Canada, Los Angeles, Phoenix, and way to many other places too numerous to count.

It was all just a get down for the get down, get down for the get down, a get down for the get down ride. I had so much fun, you wouldn't believe it, unless you were there, like my muse was.

And let me tell you, there is never going to be anything like being young, with a whole lot of money, nothing like it ever.

All praises to God and much love and praise to all those who helped me and much love to all those I helped. It was a wild ride, a joyful ride, a creative business ride, a beautiful ride.

Tony Rose
May 2018

**ME WITH THREE OF MY FOUR SONS WITH SYLVIA
AT SYLVIA'S RESTAURANT, HARLEM / NEW YORK CITY, 2004**

MY OLDEST SON, 2014

**TONY ROSE WITH FRIENDS, KENDALL MINTER, ESQ.
AND MAURICE STARR, PHOENIX AZ 2007**

TONY ROSE, PRESIDENT SOLID PLATINUM RECORDS AND PRODUCTIONS AND MAURICE STARR, PRESIDENT, BOSTON INTERNATIONAL RECORDS, 1989

TONY ROSE WITH FRIENDS LARRY JOSEPH AND PRINCE CHARLES ALEXANDER, ROXBURY (BOSTON) MA, 2012

TONY ROSE WITH MY GREAT FRIEND, THE FIRST LADY OF ROXBURY (BOSTON) JOURNALISM, KAY BOURNE. HER WORK IS RESPONSIBLE FOR THE SUCCESS OF MY AND HUNDREDS OF MUSICIANS, WRITERS, SINGERS, DANCERS, ARTISTS, ACTORS, IN THE MUSIC, DANCE, THEATER, TELEVISION, FILM, AND ART WORLDS FROM ROXBURY. (BOSTON), MA. 2015

TONY ROSE BOOK CATALOG AND MUSIC DISCOGRAPHY

TONY ROSE, PUBLISHER/CEO,
AMBER COMMUNICATIONS GROUP, INC.

TONY ROSE BOOKS AND MUSIC

WWW.AMBERBOOKSPUBLISHING.COM

WWW.TONYROSEENTERPRISES.COM

NICKI MINAJ - BIOGRAPHY

https://www.youtube.com/watch?v=2yvFB5_jdFA
Amazon.com Paperback
www.amberbookspublishing.com

SUGE KNIGHT - BIOGRAPHY

https://www.youtube.com/watch?v=jQE67ecpx6U
Barnes&Noble.com Paperback
www.amberbookspublishing.com

RICK JAMES - BIOGRAPHY

https://www.youtube.com/watch?v=EU74aeWrS_8
Barnes&Noble.com Paperback
www.amberbookspublishing.com

R. KELLY - BIOGRAPHY

https://www.youtube.com/watch?v=jQE67ecpx6U
Amazon.com Paperback
www.amberbookspublishing.com

PRINCE: IN THE STUDIO - BIOGRAPHY

https://www.youtube.com/watch?v=hd_52k7_ALw
Barnes&Noble.com Paperback
www.amberbookspublishing.com

OL' DIRTY BASTARD - BIOGRAPHY
https://www.youtube.com/watch?v=uxuaCz-W2vY
Amazon.com Paperback
www.amberbookspublishing.com

NEW KIDS ON THE BLOCK - BIOGRAPHY
https://www.youtube.com/watch?v=KIkHNbYw1Yk
Amazon.com
Barnes&Noble.com Paperback
www.amberbookspublishing.com

MICHAEL JACKSON - BIOGRAPHY
https://www.youtube.com/watch?v=AqrO1s8wm0Q
Michael Jackson
Amberbk@aol.com For Paperback

LL COOL J - VARIOUS RAP ARTISTS BIOGRAPHIES
https://www.youtube.com/watch?v=-82opWhPSek
Amazon.com Paperback
www.amberbookspublishing.com

LIL WAYNE - BIOGRAPHY
https://www.youtube.com/watch?v=Ux1DM70ASuc
Barnes&Noble.com Paperback
www.amberbookspublishing.com

LADY GAGA - BIOGRAPHY
https://www.youtube.com/watch?v=sWNjhQnO1qY
Amazon.com Paperback
www.amberbookspublishing.com

KANYE WEST - BIOGRAPHY

https://www.youtube.com/watch?v=NETkocemK4E

KANYE WEST - BIOGRAPHY

https://www.youtube.com/watch?v=kpjE3q4iYoQ
Amazon.com Paperback
www.amberbookspublishing.com

JAY Z - BIOGRAPHY

https://www.youtube.com/watch?v=-rTC70hj44U
Barnes&Noble.com Paperback
www.amberbookspublishing.com

HAL JACKSON - BIOGRAPHY

https://www.youtube.com/watch?v=9hatzBMf800
Amazon.com Paperback
www.amberbookspublishing.com

GEORGE CLINTON - BIOGRAPHY

https://www.youtube.com/watch?v=5Jv2JJfVWi8
Amazon.com Paperback
Barnes&Noble.com Paperback
www.amberbookspublishing.com

EMINEM - BIOGRAPHY

https://www.youtube.com/watch?v=gEQF8co-Vjg
Amazon.com Paperback
www.amberbookspublishing.com

EMINEM AND DR. DRE - BIOGRAPHY

https://www.youtube.com/watch?v=CHJYb1JtKHg
Amazon.com Paperback
www.amberbookspublishing.com

DR. DRE: IN THE STUDIO - BIOGRAPHY
https://www.youtube.com/watch?v=WeiAhZpaNW0
Amazon.com Paperback
www.amberbookspublishing.com

ALICIA KEYS, ASHANTI, BEYONCE, DESTINY'S CHILD, JENNIFER LOPEZ - BIOGRAPHY
https://www.youtube.com/watch?v=VKJa7bLVwsQ
Amazon.com Paperback
www.amberbookspublishing.com

DESTINY'S CHILD - BIOGRAPHY
https://www.youtube.com/watch?v=I72sBTeCCJc
Amberbk@aol.com
For Product

CHRISTINA AGUILERA - BIOGRAPHY
https://www.youtube.com/watch?v=EoaxD2lhKCk
Amazon.com Paperback
www.amberbookspublishing.com

RED HOT CHILI PEPPERS - BIOGRAPHY
https://www.youtube.com/watch?v=rhCrE-1iUrU
Amazon.com Paperback
www.amberbookspublishing.com

BLACK EYED PEAS - BIOGRAPHY
https://www.youtube.com/watch?v=5RNBuF1T5Wk
Amazon.com Paperback
www.amberbookspublishing.com

NOTORIUS B.I.G. BIGGIE SMALLS - BIOGRAPHY
https://www.youtube.com/watch?v=fTcSoWxZBto
Barnes&Noble.com Paperback
www.amberbookspublishing.com

BEYONCE - BIOGRAPHY
https://www.youtube.com/watch?v=vPPPP_wP2IE
Amazon.com Paperback
www.amberbookspublishing.com

AMY WINEHOUSE - BIOGRAPHY
https://www.youtube.com/watch?v=e80XZgSRj0w
Barnes&Noble.comPaperback
www.amberbookspublishing.com

AALIYAH - BIOGRAPHY
https://www.youtube.com/watch?v=WZyBgnsDQ2g
Amazon.com Kindle
www.amberbookspublishing.com

FIFTY CENT - BIOGRAPHY
https://www.youtube.com/watch?v=ZUPmdzeNnXs
Barnes&Noble.com Paperback
www.amberbookspublishing.com

TUPAC SHAKUR - BIOGRAPHY
https://www.youtube.com/watch?v=h1rHULMm9bM
Barnes&Noble.com Paperback
www.amberbookspublishing.com

YOGA & MEDITATION BOOK FOR AFRICAN AMERICANS.

https://www.youtube.com/watch?v=vZYrQsERHlQ
Amazon.com Paperback
www.amberbookspublishing.com

**WAVEY, CURLY, KINKY -
AFRICAN AMERICAN CHILD'S HAIR CARE GUIDE.**

https://www.youtube.com/watch?v=uv_ax2jkFpA
Barnes&Noble.com
www.amberbookspublishing.com

**WAKE UP AND SMELL THE DOLLARS
- MONEY BOOK FOR AFRICAN AMERICANS.**

https://www.youtube.com/watch?v=KfyGOQa9SM4
Amazon.com Paperback
www.amberbookspublishing.com

URBAN SUICIDE: DRUG CRISIS IN BLACK AMERICA.

https://www.youtube.com/watch?v=ec2iqUBHtRE
Barnes&Noble.com Nook
www.amberbookspublishing.com

SPORTS AND ATHLETIC SCHOLARSHIP BOOK.

https://www.youtube.com/watch?v=AU8mRvP2tZM
Contact
Amberbk@aol.com
for Paperback
www.amberbookspublishing.com

REAL ESTATE AND WEALTH BOOK FOR AFRICAN AMERICANS.

https://www.youtube.com/watch?v=90c9XFlRpr0
Amazon.com Paperback
www.amberbookspublishing.com

PAY YOURSELF FIRST
- FINANCIAL BOOK FOR AFRICAN AMERICANS.

https://www.youtube.com/watch?v=65oCZ_i_YxU
Amazon.com Paperback
www.amberbookspublishing.com

PRESIDENT OBAMA TALKS BACK
- NAACP IMAGE AWARD WINNING BOOK.

https://www.youtube.com/watch?v=ISV9TopgClQ
Amazon.com Paperback
www.amberbookspublishing.com

NO MISTAKES - BOOK FOR AFRICAN AMERICAN TEENAGERS.

https://www.youtube.com/watch?v=oa9gTXW1hl0
Amazon.com Kindle
www.amberbookspublishing.com

LITERARY DIVAS
- THE TOP 100 AFRICAN AMERICAN WOMEN IN LITERTURE.

https://www.youtube.com/watch?v=edNhO2ZjpwM
Contact
Amberbk@aol.com
For Product
www.amberbookspublishing.com

THE INVESTIGATION AND STUDY OF THE WHITE PEOPLE OF AMERICA AND WESTERN EUROPE.

https://www.youtube.com/watch?v=w7mdxHAPxZg
Avilailable on Amazon
www.amberbookspublishing.com

IS MODELING FOR YOU?
THE BOOK FOR YOUNG ASPIRING BLACK MODELS.

https://www.youtube.com/watch?v=Vo7052BtEAs
Amazon.com Paperback
www.amberbookspublishing.com

MUSIC INSTRUCTION GUIDE FOR PIANO.

https://www.youtube.com/watch?v=wMSpay3WKuw
Amazon.com Paperback
www.amberbookspublishing.com

COLLEGE PREPARATION BOOK FOR AFRICAN AMERICANS.

https://www.youtube.com/watch?v=sEfcAOejAa8
Contact
Amberbk@aol.com
for Paperback
www.amberbookspublishing.com

HOW TO GET RICH
- AFRICAN AMERICAN GUIDE TO GAINING WEALTH.

https://www.youtube.com/watch?v=ngfnh_aZMzQ
Amazon.com Paperback
www.amberbookspublishing.com

RECORD PRODUCERS, SONGWRITERS, HOW TO BE IN THE MUSIC BIZ.

https://www.youtube.com/watch?v=SW_e_DfPZ6k
Amazon.com Paperback
www.amberbookspublishing.com

HOW TO BE AN ENTREPRENEUR AND KEEP YOUR SANITY.

https://www.youtube.com/watch?v=81-abqLYXNE
Amazon.com Paperback
www.amberbookspublishing.com

HOME DAY CARE BOOK FOR AFRICAN AMERICANS

https://www.youtube.com/watch?v=fyHu-lWV4Sw
Barnes&Noble.com Nook
www.amberbookspublishing.com

GET THAT CUTIE IN COMMERCIALS.

https://www.youtube.com/watch?v=gnTJgNpk7Gg
Amazon.com Paperback
www.amberbookspublishing.com

MAKEUP AND SKIN CARE BOOK FOR AFRICAN AMERICAN TEENAGERS.

https://www.youtube.com/watch?v=GnU1a3uiVd4
Barnes&Noble.com Paperback
www.amberbookspublishing.com

THE BLACK PERSONS GUIDE TO WORKING OUTSIDE OF CORPORATE AMERICA

https://www.youtube.com/watch?v=zN5DoseF_8A
Amazon.com Paperback
www.amberbookspublishing.com

BEAUTIFUL BLACK HAIR BOOK BY SHAMBOOSIE

https://www.youtube.com/watch?v=JAvbiFMwbPk
Barnes&Noble.com Paperback
www.amberbookspublishing.com

MICHELLE OBAMA
- BESIDE EVERY GREAT MAN, IS A GREAT WOMAN.

https://www.youtube.com/watch?v=OafqPEt1F8o
Contact
Amberbk@aol.com
For Paperback
www.amberbookspublishing.com

THE AUTOBIOGRAPHY OF AN AMERICAN GHETTO BOY.

https://www.youtube.com/watch?v=meOjEOc0u8M
Amazon.com Kindle
Amazon.com Paperback
www.amberbookspublishing.com

AMERICA: THE BLACK POINT OF VIEW

https://www.youtube.com/watch?v=89tEDPoz0BQ
Amazon
www.amberbookspublishing.com

AGELESS BEAUTY:
MAKEUP AND SKIN CARE BOOK FOR WOMEN AND TEENS.

https://www.youtube.com/watch?v=unMX2OOzNL0
Amazon.com Paperback
www.amberbookspublishing.com

AFROCENTRIC BRIDE: A BRIDAL BOOK FOR WOMEN OF COLOR.

https://www.youtube.com/watch?v=1Qa-0yVENNI
Contact
Amberbk@aol.com
for paperback
www.amberbookspublishing.com

HOW TO SELF-PUBLISH YOUR BOOK AND BE SUCCESSFUL

https://www.youtube.com/watch?v=jt72h3F59cI
Amazon.com Paperback
www.amberbookspublishing.com

THE TRAVEL GUIDE BOOK FOR AFRICAN AMERICANS

https://www.youtube.com/watch?v=keZKC0ieRJo
Barnes&Noble.com Paperback
www.amberbookspublishing.com

THE AFRICAN AMERICAN TEENAGERS GUIDE BOOK.

https://www.youtube.com/watch?v=RYaKOae4NyM
Amazon.com Paperback
www.amberbookspublishing.com

THE AFRICAN AMERICAN SCHOLARSHIP GUIDE BOOK.

https://www.youtube.com/watch?v=BeowNpVqCtk
Amazon.com Paperback
www.amberbookspublishing.com

HURRICANE KATRINA AND NEW ORLEANS REVISITED.

https://www.youtube.com/watch?v=-HFZTyAFK-A
Amazon.com Kindle
www.amberbookspublishing.com

REAL ESTATE INVESTING
GUIDE BOOK FOR AFRICAN AMERICANS.
https://www.youtube.com/watch?v=CcGIEM4fA_4
Amazon.com Paperback
www.amberbookspublishing.com

AFRICAN AMERICAN GUIDE BOOK TO TRACING OUR ROOTS
https://www.youtube.com/watch?v=QA5jvMNSOKc
Amazon.com Paperback
www.amberbookspublishing.com

THE AFRICAN AMERICAN EMPLOYMENT GUIDE.
https://www.youtube.com/watch?v=eA-WxOXCb8w
Amazon.com Paperback
www.amberbookspublishing.com

THE AFRICAN AMERICAN CRIMINAL JUSTICE GUIDE.
https://www.youtube.com/watch?v=dOfL4YPGRR8
Amazon.com Paperback
www.amberbookspublishing.com

THE AFRICAN AMERICAN WOMAN'S
GUIDE TO SUCCESSFUL MAKEUP.
https://www.youtube.com/watch?v=2yvFB5_jdFA
Amazon.com Paperback
www.amberbookspublishing.com

THE AFRICAN AMERICAN WOMAN'S
GUIDE TO MAKEUP AND SKIN CARE.
https://www.youtube.com/watch?v=I69n2OdIYss
Amazon.com Paperback
www.amberbookspublishing.com

AFRICAN AMERICAN HISTORY IN THE UNITED STATES OF AMERICA

https://www.youtube.com/watch?v=6bdE-6_y7b4
Barnes&Noble.com Paperback
www.amberbookspublishing.com

101 REAL MONEY QUESTIONS: AFRICAN AMERICAN FINANCIAL BOOK.

https://www.youtube.com/watch?v=ygnFOVcEDr8
Amazon.com Paperback.
www.amberbookspublishing.com

TONY ROSE MUSIC DISCOGRAPHY

MUSIC RECORDED, EXECUTIVE PRODUCED, PRODUCED, WRITTEN OR CO-WRITTEN BY TONY ROSE

WWW.TONYROSEENTERPRISES.COM

LOS ANGELES

1975

ROBBIE HILLS FAMILY AFFAIR

YES I KNOW

https://www.youtube.com/watch?v=8WKlnnyKrkI

LOS ANGELES

1975

ROBBIE HILLS FAMILY AFFAIR

REINCARNATION

https://www.youtube.com/watch?v=rIA61xYd_hc

BOSTON

1979

PRINCE CHARLES AND THE CITY BEAT BAND

IN THE STREETS

https://www.youtube.com/watch?v=iOY3eSkHxH4
https://store.cdbaby.com/cd/princecharlesthecitybeat

BOSTON

1980

PRINCE CHARLES AND THE CITY BEAT BAND

RISE (MOVE YOUR FEET TO THE BEST)

https://www.youtube.com/watch?v=JoCeZIbWpls&t=6s
https://store.cdbaby.com/cd/princecharlesthecitybeat

PRINCE CHARLES AND THE CITY BEAT BAND
YOU ARE MY LOVE
https://www.youtube.com/watch?v=P2xdgUyH1YM
https://store.cdbaby.com/cd/princecharlesthecitybeat

PRINCE CHARLES AND THE CITY BEAT BAND
PASSION
https://www.youtube.com/watch?v=1pgtgbvDjO0
https://store.cdbaby.com/cd/princecharlesthecitybeat

PRINCE CHARLES AND THE CITY BEAT BAND
IN THE STREETS
https://www.youtube.com/watch?v=iOY3eSkHxH4
https://store.cdbaby.com/cd/princecharlesthecitybeat

PRINCE CHARLES AND THE CITY BEAT BAND
TIGHT JEANS
https://www.youtube.com/watch?v=Hr5e0Qd25Xc
https://store.cdbaby.com/cd/princecharlesthecitybeat

PRINCE CHARLES AND THE CITY BEAT BAND
DONT GO AWAY
https://www.youtube.com/watch?v=Hr7sQjwz1xw
https://store.cdbaby.com/cd/princecharlesthecitybeat

NEW YORK CITY

1981

SLYCK
LOVE IT OR (BEAT THE BUSH) DJ SPINNA MIX
https://www.youtube.com/watch?v=x9ZriqYyKJs
https://store.cdbaby.com/cd/princecharlesandthecityb

SLYCK
BUSH BEAT (12" INSTRUMENTAL ORIGINAL MIX)
https://www.youtube.com/watch?v=ZN20wZoPHbE&t=57s
https://store.cdbaby.com/cd/princecharlesandthecityb

BOSTON
1982
KEVIN FLEETWOOD AND THE CADILLACS OF SOUND
SWEAT IT OFF
https://www.youtube.com/watch?v=mSVNijHS2_M

KEVIN FLEETWOOD AND THE CADILLACS OF SOUND
https://www.youtube.com/watch?v=egO8IfGmE7w

NEW YORK CITY
1982
IMAGE
YOU'RE MY ONLY DESIRE
https://www.youtube.com/watch?v=-5_SxaYnA2g

NEW YORK CITY
1982
PRINCE CHARLES AND THE CITY BEAT BAND
VIDEO FREAK (DEFEND IT) TONY ROSE MIX
https://www.youtube.com/watch?v=uAMlZtI2tk0&t=185s
https://store.cdbaby.com/cd/princecharlesandthecityb

PRINCE CHARLES AND THE CITY BEAT BAND
VIDEO FREAK (DEFEND IT) RADIO MIX
https://www.youtube.com/watch?v=mklzkLoChlY
https://store.cdbaby.com/cd/princecharlesandthecityb

BOSTON AND NEW YORK CITY
1982 - 1983
PRINCE CHARLES AND THE CITY BEAT BAND
CASH, CASH MONEY
https://www.youtube.com/watch?v=
https://store.cdbaby.com/cd/princecharlesthecitybeat

PRINCE CHARLES AND THE CITY BEAT BAND
DON'T FAKE THE FUNK
https://www.youtube.com/watch?v=2m5_TEF47LA
https://store.cdbaby.com/cd/princecharlesthecitybeat

PRINCE CHARLES AND THE CITY BEAT BAND
BIG CHESTED GIRLS
https://www.youtube.com/watch?v=V5JkArRQ9UI
https://store.cdbaby.com/cd/princecharlesthecitybeat

PRINCE CHARLES AND THE CITY BEAT BAND
COLD AS ICE
https://www.youtube.com/watch?v=87tKKFax_E8
https://store.cdbaby.com/cd/princecharlesthecitybeat

PRINCE CHARLES AND THE CITY BEAT BAND
I'M A FOOL FOR LOVE
https://www.youtube.com/watch?v=DUXirFYqba0&t=3s
https://store.cdbaby.com/cd/princecharlesandthecityb

PRINCE CHARLES AND THE CITY BEAT BAND
JUNGLE STOMP
https://www.youtube.com/watch?v=FVrvrkHDZ6M&t=3s
https://store.cdbaby.com/cd/princecharlesandthecityb

PRINCE CHARLES AND THE CITY BEAT BAND
LOVE IT OR (BEAT THE BUSH) PRINCE CHARLES VIRGIN REMIX
https://www.youtube.com/watch?v=L4UkWwMovR4
https://store.cdbaby.com/cd/princecharlesandthecityb

NEW YORK CITY
1983 - 1984
PRINCE CHARLES AND THE CITY BEAT BAND
STONE COLD KILLERS
https://www.youtube.com/watch?v=O5QUbKkDgRo
https://store.cdbaby.com/cd/princecharlesthecitybeat

PRINCE CHARLES AND THE CITY BEAT BAND
SKINTIGHT TINA
https://www.youtube.com/watch?v=yUQIv-E7IRA
https://store.cdbaby.com/cd/princecharlesthecitybeat

PRINCE CHARLES AND THE CITY BEAT BAND
I NEED YOU
https://www.youtube.com/watch?v=1ep470dazWw
https://store.cdbaby.com/cd/princecharlesthecitybeat

PRINCE CHARLES AND THE CITY BEAT BAND
MORE MONEY
https://www.youtube.com/watch?v=JqAyclAb-qI
https://store.cdbaby.com/cd/princecharlesthecitybeat

PRINCE CHARLES AND THE CITY BEAT BAND
FISTFUL OF DOLLARS
https://www.youtube.com/watch?v=ClMx5jyt5Ao
https://store.cdbaby.com/cd/princecharlesthecitybeat

PRINCE CHARLES AND THE CITY BEAT BAND
CITY LIFE
https://www.youtube.com/watch?v=FRp447EjWeY
https://store.cdbaby.com/cd/princecharlesthecitybeat

PRINCE CHARLES AND THE CITY BEAT BAND
COMBAT ZONE
https://www.youtube.com/watch?v=IAiCEMDO1FI&t=182s
https://store.cdbaby.com/cd/princecharlesthecitybeat

PRINCE CHARLES AND THE CITY BEAT BAND
I WANNA SATISFY YOU
https://www.youtube.com/watch?v=op25KoLZM1k
https://store.cdbaby.com/cd/princecharlesthecitybeat

PRINCE CHARLES AND THE CITY BEAT BAND
LONG DISTANT LOVER
https://www.youtube.com/watch?v=dSzk2d5KiH0
https://store.cdbaby.com/cd/princecharlesthecitybeat

BOSTON

1985

OMAR D.
BORN TO BE FREE
https://www.youtube.com/watch?v=XKrG1Cgmaug

OMAR D.
DON'T FALL BACK
https://www.youtube.com/watch?v=cEK4tvFgA_A

BOSTON

1985

TANYA HART
RED BIRD
https://www.youtube.com/watch?v=ZWZc1VeFnFg

NEW YORK CITY
1985 -1986
PRINCE CHARLES AND THE CITY BEAT BAND
WE CAN MAKE IT HAPPEN
https://www.youtube.com/watch?v=1aAvJcqGj7g
https://store.cdbaby.com/cd/princecharlesandthecityb

NEW YORK CITY
1986
PRINCE CHARLES AND THE CITY BEAT BAND
I CAN'T STOP LOVING YOU
https://www.youtube.com/watch?v=WEBN66_1uYs
https://store.cdbaby.com/cd/princecharlesandthecityb

NEW YORK CITY
1987
PRINCE CHARLES AND THE CITY BEAT BAND
I'LL BE THERE FOR YOU
https://www.youtube.com/watch?v=AagIgK6QDNM
https://store.cdbaby.com/cd/princecharlesandthecityb

NEW YORK CITY AND BOSTON
1987
THE COMING ATTRACTION
BE MY LADY
https://www.youtube.com/watch?v=ydJZdoPs9L4
https://www.youtube.com/watch?v=F-n5hHKpUho

BOSTON
1989
NEW KIDS ON THE BLOCK
MERRY, MERRY CHRISTMAS
https://www.youtube.com/watch?v=XLMJG407SjI

BOSTON
1989
NEW KIDS ON THE BLOCK
I STILL BELIEVE IN SANTA CLAUS
https://www.youtube.com/watch?v=WQsCkDfMj2E

BOSTON
1989
NEW KIDS ON THE BLOCK
LAST NIGHT I SAW SANTA CLAUS
https://www.youtube.com/watch?v=b2s41GOtWEc

BOSTON
1989
NEW KIDS ON THE BLOCK
THIS ONE'S FOR THE CHILDREN
https://www.youtube.com/watch?v=oc12pZoJdgc

BOSTON
1989
NEW KIDS ON THE BLOCK
THIS ONE'S FOR THE CHILDREN (RE-PRISE)
https://www.youtube.com/watch?v=3-i-0SBR8YI

NEW YORK CITY
1991
CANTOR COHEN DEBORAH
REGGAE DOWN BABYLON
https://www.youtube.com/watch?v=OMeKu623_gQ&t=38s

NEW YORK CITY
1991-1992
WHITE GIRLS WITH SOUL
CONEY ISLAND BOUND
https://www.youtube.com/watch?v=t20DPSoUULM&t=111s
https://store.cdbaby.com/cd/whitegirlswithsoul

WHITE GIRLS WITH SOUL
FUNKY FUNKY, WHITE GIRLS
https://www.youtube.com/watch?v=FRumtxhW0O4
https://store.cdbaby.com/cd/whitegirlswithsoul

WHITE GIRLS WITH SOUL
AMERIKA DO BEAUTIFUL
https://www.youtube.com/watch?v=Dp9q9fly4Uk
https://store.cdbaby.com/cd/whitegirlswithsoul

WHITE GIRLS WITH SOUL
WHISPERS!
https://www.youtube.com/watch?v=aHE5rKIyrIg
https://store.cdbaby.com/cd/whitegirlswithsoul

WHITE GIRLS WITH SOUL
HOW'D YA LIKE THIS!
https://store.cdbaby.com/cd/whitegirlswithsoul

WHITE GIRLS WITH SOUL
YOU JUST CAN'T HAVE IT!
https://www.youtube.com/watch?v=WgceJNytxok
https://store.cdbaby.com/cd/whitegirlswithsoul

WHITE GIRLS WITH SOUL
FOR YOU
https://www.youtube.com/watch?v=P0s-Y6UjvE4
https://store.cdbaby.com/cd/whitegirlswithsoul

WHITE GIRLS WITH SOUL
GO WHITE GIRLS GO WHITE GIRLS GO
https://www.youtube.com/watch?v=ueXHUZh6buY
https://store.cdbaby.com/cd/whitegirlswithsoul

NEW YORK CITY
1994
VALI ROSE
IT'S A SHAME
https://www.youtube.com/watch?v=nbxi7Cw1kBA

NEW YORK CITY
2006-2007
MR. PETERSON
FOREVER
https://www.youtube.com/watch?v=43GbKBxx0Tk
https://store.cdbaby.com/cd/mrpeterson

MR. PETERSON
DIME GIRL
https://www.youtube.com/watch?v=LGkDkEjrxpY
https://store.cdbaby.com/cd/mrpeterson

MR. PETERSON
HOLLA
https://www.youtube.com/watch?v=D-dcV-zH1SU
https://store.cdbaby.com/cd/mrpeterson

MR. PETERSON
FATHER
https://www.youtube.com/watch?v=wAf52J3B5xk
https://store.cdbaby.com/cd/mrpeterson

MR. PETERSON
DO IT AGAIN
https://www.youtube.com/watch?v=j_Yj9JpYelk
https://store.cdbaby.com/cd/mrpeterson

MR. PETERSON
MAMA RAISED US
https://www.youtube.com/watch?v=s75hsVHGP4k&t=82s
https://store.cdbaby.com/cd/mrpeterson

MR. PETERSON
KICKIN IT
https://www.youtube.com/watch?v=bjPjAtsBpbY
https://store.cdbaby.com/cd/mrpeterson

MR. PETERSON
GET FRESH
https://www.youtube.com/watch?v=NpNt712qGg8
https://store.cdbaby.com/cd/mrpeterson

MR. PETERSON
OFF THE CHAIN
https://www.youtube.com/watch?v=YhIQKBMvrf8
https://store.cdbaby.com/cd/mrpeterson

MR. PETERSON
YOU'RE ALL I NEED
https://www.youtube.com/watch?v=iIIsHrNf218
https://store.cdbaby.com/cd/mrpeterson

PHOENIX

2009

GEE - T

OUT OF THIS WORLD

https://www.youtube.com/watch?v=F7jUM81Sryc

https://store.cdbaby.com/cd/geet

PHOENIX

2009

GEE - T

FRIEND

https://www.youtube.com/watch?v=w7LXJxqEWLM

https://store.cdbaby.com/cd/geet

PHOENIX

2009

GEE - T

LAMEZ

https://www.youtube.com/watch?v=BH7mIhw-OIw

https://store.cdbaby.com/cd/geet

PHOENIX

2009

GEE - T

WEIRD

https://www.youtube.com/watch?v=y0kamPyz1hA

https://store.cdbaby.com/cd/geet

BOSTON

2012

PRINCE TAJ420

WHAT IS YOUR NAME

https://www.youtube.com/watch?v=zwVEgQO2UUo

https://store.cdbaby.com/cd/princetaj420

ENTERTAINMENT BOOKS
BY TONY ROSE

RECORD PRODUCER

MUSIC PUBLISHER

RECORD COMPANY

PERSONAL MANAGER

FILM PRODUCER

BOOK PUBLISHER

SOLD AT:
WWW.AMAZON.COM
WWW.BARNES&NOBLE.COM
WWW.HOW2BEBOOKS.COM

HOW TO BE IN THE ENTERTAINMENT BUSINESS
By Tony Rose

WWW.TONYROSEENTERPRISES.COM
WWW.AMBERBOOKSPUBLISHING.COM
WWW.QUALITYPRESS.INFO

VIEW ALL AMBER BOOKS AT:
WWW.AMBERBOOKSPUBLISHING.COM
Call: 602-743-7211 / Email: amberbk@aol.com

WWW.TONYROSEENTERPRISES.COM

www.ingramcontent.com/pod-product-compliance
Lightning Source LLC
Chambersburg PA
CBHW071728080526
44588CB00013B/1946